Mometrix
TEST PREPARATION

CLEP®

American Government Exam Secrets Study Guide

Dear Future Exam Success Story

First of all, **THANK YOU** for purchasing Mometrix study materials!

Second, congratulations! You are one of the few determined test-takers who are committed to doing whatever it takes to excel on your exam. **You have come to the right place.** We developed these study materials with one goal in mind: to deliver you the information you need in a format that's concise and easy to use.

In addition to optimizing your guide for the content of the test, we've outlined our recommended steps for breaking down the preparation process into small, attainable goals so you can make sure you stay on track.

We've also analyzed the entire test-taking process, identifying the most common pitfalls and showing how you can overcome them and be ready for any curveball the test throws you.

Standardized testing is one of the biggest obstacles on your road to success, which only increases the importance of doing well in the high-pressure, high-stakes environment of test day. Your results on this test could have a significant impact on your future, and this guide provides the information and practical advice to help you achieve your full potential on test day.

Your success is our success

We would love to hear from you! If you would like to share the story of your exam success or if you have any questions or comments in regard to our products, please contact us at **800-673-8175** or **support@mometrix.com**.

Thanks again for your business and we wish you continued success!

Sincerely,
The Mometrix Test Preparation Team

Need more help? Check out our flashcards at:
http://MometrixFlashcards.com/CLEP

TABLE OF CONTENTS

Introduction

Thank you for purchasing this resource! You have made the choice to prepare yourself for a test that could have a huge impact on your future, and this guide is designed to help you be fully ready for test day. Obviously, it's important to have a solid understanding of the test material, but you also need to be prepared for the unique environment and stressors of the test, so that you can perform to the best of your abilities.

For this purpose, the first section that appears in this guide is the **Secret Keys**. We've devoted countless hours to meticulously researching what works and what doesn't, and we've boiled down our findings to the five most impactful steps you can take to improve your performance on the test. We start at the beginning with study planning and move through the preparation process, all the way to the testing strategies that will help you get the most out of what you know when you're finally sitting in front of the test.

We recommend that you start preparing for your test as far in advance as possible. However, if you've bought this guide as a last-minute study resource and only have a few days before your test, we recommend that you skip over the first two Secret Keys since they address a long-term study plan.

If you struggle with **test anxiety**, we strongly encourage you to check out our recommendations for how you can overcome it. Test anxiety is a formidable foe, but it can be beaten, and we want to make sure you have the tools you need to defeat it.

Secret Key #1 – Plan Big, Study Small

There's a lot riding on your performance. If you want to ace this test, you're going to need to keep your skills sharp and the material fresh in your mind. You need a plan that lets you review everything you need to know while still fitting in your schedule. We'll break this strategy down into three categories.

Information Organization

Start with the information you already have: the official test outline. From this, you can make a complete list of all the concepts you need to cover before the test. Organize these concepts into groups that can be studied together, and create a list of any related vocabulary you need to learn so you can brush up on any difficult terms. You'll want to keep this vocabulary list handy once you actually start studying since you may need to add to it along the way.

Time Management

Once you have your set of study concepts, decide how to spread them out over the time you have left before the test. Break your study plan into small, clear goals so you have a manageable task for each day and know exactly what you're doing. Then just focus on one small step at a time. When you manage your time this way, you don't need to spend hours at a time studying. Studying a small block of content for a short period each day helps you retain information better and avoid stressing over how much you have left to do. You can relax knowing that you have a plan to cover everything in time. In order for this strategy to be effective though, you have to start studying early and stick to your schedule. Avoid the exhaustion and futility that comes from last-minute cramming!

Study Environment

The environment you study in has a big impact on your learning. Studying in a coffee shop, while probably more enjoyable, is not likely to be as fruitful as studying in a quiet room. It's important to keep distractions to a minimum. You're only planning to study for a short block of time, so make the most of it. Don't pause to check your phone or get up to find a snack. It's also important to **avoid multitasking**. Research has consistently shown that multitasking will make your studying dramatically less effective. Your study area should also be comfortable and well-lit so you don't have the distraction of straining your eyes or sitting on an uncomfortable chair.

The time of day you study is also important. You want to be rested and alert. Don't wait until just before bedtime. Study when you'll be most likely to comprehend and remember. Even better, if you know what time of day your test will be, set that time aside for study. That way your brain will be used to working on that subject at that specific time and you'll have a better chance of recalling information.

Finally, it can be helpful to team up with others who are studying for the same test. Your actual studying should be done in as isolated an environment as possible, but the work of organizing the information and setting up the study plan can be divided up. In between study sessions, you can discuss with your teammates the concepts that you're all studying and quiz each other on the details. Just be sure that your teammates are as serious about the test as you are. If you find that your study time is being replaced with social time, you might need to find a new team.

Secret Key #2 – Make Your Studying Count

You're devoting a lot of time and effort to preparing for this test, so you want to be absolutely certain it will pay off. This means doing more than just reading the content and hoping you can remember it on test day. It's important to make every minute of study count. There are two main areas you can focus on to make your studying count.

Retention

It doesn't matter how much time you study if you can't remember the material. You need to make sure you are retaining the concepts. To check your retention of the information you're learning, try recalling it at later times with minimal prompting. Try carrying around flashcards and glance at one or two from time to time or ask a friend who's also studying for the test to quiz you.

To enhance your retention, look for ways to put the information into practice so that you can apply it rather than simply recalling it. If you're using the information in practical ways, it will be much easier to remember. Similarly, it helps to solidify a concept in your mind if you're not only reading it to yourself but also explaining it to someone else. Ask a friend to let you teach them about a concept you're a little shaky on (or speak aloud to an imaginary audience if necessary). As you try to summarize, define, give examples, and answer your friend's questions, you'll understand the concepts better and they will stay with you longer. Finally, step back for a big picture view and ask yourself how each piece of information fits with the whole subject. When you link the different concepts together and see them working together as a whole, it's easier to remember the individual components.

Finally, practice showing your work on any multi-step problems, even if you're just studying. Writing out each step you take to solve a problem will help solidify the process in your mind, and you'll be more likely to remember it during the test.

Modality

Modality simply refers to the means or method by which you study. Choosing a study modality that fits your own individual learning style is crucial. No two people learn best in exactly the same way, so it's important to know your strengths and use them to your advantage.

For example, if you learn best by visualization, focus on visualizing a concept in your mind and draw an image or a diagram. Try color-coding your notes, illustrating them, or creating symbols that will trigger your mind to recall a learned concept. If you learn best by hearing or discussing information, find a study partner who learns the same way or read aloud to yourself. Think about how to put the information in your own words. Imagine that you are giving a lecture on the topic and record yourself so you can listen to it later.

For any learning style, flashcards can be helpful. Organize the information so you can take advantage of spare moments to review. Underline key words or phrases. Use different colors for different categories. Mnemonic devices (such as creating a short list in which every item starts with the same letter) can also help with retention. Find what works best for you and use it to store the information in your mind most effectively and easily.

Secret Key #3 – Practice the Right Way

Your success on test day depends not only on how many hours you put into preparing, but also on whether you prepared the right way. It's good to check along the way to see if your studying is paying off. One of the most effective ways to do this is by taking practice tests to evaluate your progress. Practice tests are useful because they show exactly where you need to improve. Every time you take a practice test, pay special attention to these three groups of questions:

- The questions you got wrong
- The questions you had to guess on, even if you guessed right
- The questions you found difficult or slow to work through

This will show you exactly what your weak areas are, and where you need to devote more study time. Ask yourself why each of these questions gave you trouble. Was it because you didn't understand the material? Was it because you didn't remember the vocabulary? Do you need more repetitions on this type of question to build speed and confidence? Dig into those questions and figure out how you can strengthen your weak areas as you go back to review the material.

Additionally, many practice tests have a section explaining the answer choices. It can be tempting to read the explanation and think that you now have a good understanding of the concept. However, an explanation likely only covers part of the question's broader context. Even if the explanation makes perfect sense, **go back and investigate** every concept related to the question until you're positive you have a thorough understanding.

As you go along, keep in mind that the practice test is just that: practice. Memorizing these questions and answers will not be very helpful on the actual test because it is unlikely to have any of the same exact questions. If you only know the right answers to the sample questions, you won't be prepared for the real thing. **Study the concepts** until you understand them fully, and then you'll be able to answer any question that shows up on the test.

It's important to wait on the practice tests until you're ready. If you take a test on your first day of study, you may be overwhelmed by the amount of material covered and how much you need to learn. Work up to it gradually.

On test day, you'll need to be prepared for answering questions, managing your time, and using the test-taking strategies you've learned. It's a lot to balance, like a mental marathon that will have a big impact on your future. Like training for a marathon, you'll need to start slowly and work your way up. When test day arrives, you'll be ready.

Start with the strategies you've read in the first two Secret Keys—plan your course and study in the way that works best for you. If you have time, consider using multiple study resources to get different approaches to the same concepts. It can be helpful to see difficult concepts from more than one angle. Then find a good source for practice tests. Many times, the test website will suggest potential study resources or provide sample tests.

Practice Test Strategy

If you're able to find at least three practice tests, we recommend this strategy:

Untimed and Open-Book Practice

Take the first test with no time constraints and with your notes and study guide handy. Take your time and focus on applying the strategies you've learned.

Timed and Open-Book Practice

Take the second practice test open-book as well, but set a timer and practice pacing yourself to finish in time.

Timed and Closed-Book Practice

Take any other practice tests as if it were test day. Set a timer and put away your study materials. Sit at a table or desk in a quiet room, imagine yourself at the testing center, and answer questions as quickly and accurately as possible.

Keep repeating timed and closed-book tests on a regular basis until you run out of practice tests or it's time for the actual test. Your mind will be ready for the schedule and stress of test day, and you'll be able to focus on recalling the material you've learned.

Secret Key #4 – Pace Yourself

Once you're fully prepared for the material on the test, your biggest challenge on test day will be managing your time. Just knowing that the clock is ticking can make you panic even if you have plenty of time left. Work on pacing yourself so you can build confidence against the time constraints of the exam. Pacing is a difficult skill to master, especially in a high-pressure environment, so **practice is vital**.

Set time expectations for your pace based on how much time is available. For example, if a section has 60 questions and the time limit is 30 minutes, you know you have to average 30 seconds or less per question in order to answer them all. Although 30 seconds is the hard limit, set 25 seconds per question as your goal, so you reserve extra time to spend on harder questions. When you budget extra time for the harder questions, you no longer have any reason to stress when those questions take longer to answer.

Don't let this time expectation distract you from working through the test at a calm, steady pace, but keep it in mind so you don't spend too much time on any one question. Recognize that taking extra time on one question you don't understand may keep you from answering two that you do understand later in the test. If your time limit for a question is up and you're still not sure of the answer, mark it and move on, and come back to it later if the time and the test format allow. If the testing format doesn't allow you to return to earlier questions, just make an educated guess; then put it out of your mind and move on.

On the easier questions, be careful not to rush. It may seem wise to hurry through them so you have more time for the challenging ones, but it's not worth missing one if you know the concept and just didn't take the time to read the question fully. Work efficiently but make sure you understand the question and have looked at all of the answer choices, since more than one may seem right at first.

Even if you're paying attention to the time, you may find yourself a little behind at some point. You should speed up to get back on track, but do so wisely. Don't panic; just take a few seconds less on each question until you're caught up. Don't guess without thinking, but do look through the answer choices and eliminate any you know are wrong. If you can get down to two choices, it is often worthwhile to guess from those. Once you've chosen an answer, move on and don't dwell on any that you skipped or had to hurry through. If a question was taking too long, chances are it was one of the harder ones, so you weren't as likely to get it right anyway.

On the other hand, if you find yourself getting ahead of schedule, it may be beneficial to slow down a little. The more quickly you work, the more likely you are to make a careless mistake that will affect your score. You've budgeted time for each question, so don't be afraid to spend that time. Practice an efficient but careful pace to get the most out of the time you have.

Secret Key #5 – Have a Plan for Guessing

When you're taking the test, you may find yourself stuck on a question. Some of the answer choices seem better than others, but you don't see the one answer choice that is obviously correct. What do you do?

The scenario described above is very common, yet most test takers have not effectively prepared for it. Developing and practicing a plan for guessing may be one of the single most effective uses of your time as you get ready for the exam.

In developing your plan for guessing, there are three questions to address:

- When should you start the guessing process?
- How should you narrow down the choices?
- Which answer should you choose?

When to Start the Guessing Process

Unless your plan for guessing is to select C every time (which, despite its merits, is not what we recommend), you need to leave yourself enough time to apply your answer elimination strategies. Since you have a limited amount of time for each question, that means that if you're going to give yourself the best shot at guessing correctly, you have to decide quickly whether or not you will guess.

Of course, the best-case scenario is that you don't have to guess at all, so first, see if you can answer the question based on your knowledge of the subject and basic reasoning skills. Focus on the key words in the question and try to jog your memory of related topics. Give yourself a chance to bring the knowledge to mind, but once you realize that you don't have (or you can't access) the knowledge you need to answer the question, it's time to start the guessing process.

It's almost always better to start the guessing process too early than too late. It only takes a few seconds to remember something and answer the question from knowledge. Carefully eliminating wrong answer choices takes longer. Plus, going through the process of eliminating answer choices can actually help jog your memory.

Summary: Start the guessing process as soon as you decide that you can't answer the question based on your knowledge.

How to Narrow Down the Choices

The next chapter in this book (**Test-Taking Strategies**) includes a wide range of strategies for how to approach questions and how to look for answer choices to eliminate. You will definitely want to read those carefully, practice them, and figure out which ones work best for you. Here though, we're going to address a mindset rather than a particular strategy.

Your odds of guessing an answer correctly depend on how many options you are choosing from.

Number of options left	5	4	3	2	1
Odds of guessing correctly	20%	25%	33%	50%	100%

You can see from this chart just how valuable it is to be able to eliminate incorrect answers and make an educated guess, but there are two things that many test takers do that cause them to miss out on the benefits of guessing:

- Accidentally eliminating the correct answer
- Selecting an answer based on an impression

We'll look at the first one here, and the second one in the next section.

To avoid accidentally eliminating the correct answer, we recommend a thought exercise called **the $5 challenge**. In this challenge, you only eliminate an answer choice from contention if you are willing to bet $5 on it being wrong. Why $5? Five dollars is a small but not insignificant amount of money. It's an amount you could afford to lose but wouldn't want to throw away. And while losing $5 once might not hurt too much, doing it twenty times will set you back $100. In the same way, each small decision you make—eliminating a choice here, guessing on a question there—won't by itself impact your score very much, but when you put them all together, they can make a big difference. By holding each answer choice elimination decision to a higher standard, you can reduce the risk of accidentally eliminating the correct answer.

The $5 challenge can also be applied in a positive sense: If you are willing to bet $5 that an answer choice *is* correct, go ahead and mark it as correct.

Summary: Only eliminate an answer choice if you are willing to bet $5 that it is wrong.

Which Answer to Choose

You're taking the test. You've run into a hard question and decided you'll have to guess. You've eliminated all the answer choices you're willing to bet $5 on. Now you have to pick an answer. Why do we even need to talk about this? Why can't you just pick whichever one you feel like when the time comes?

The answer to these questions is that if you don't come into the test with a plan, you'll rely on your impression to select an answer choice, and if you do that, you risk falling into a trap. The test writers know that everyone who takes their test will be guessing on some of the questions, so they intentionally write wrong answer choices to seem plausible. You still have to pick an answer though, and if the wrong answer choices are designed to look right, how can you ever be sure that you're not falling for their trap? The best solution we've found to this dilemma is to take the decision out of your hands entirely. Here is the process we recommend:

Once you've eliminated any choices that you are confident (willing to bet $5) are wrong, select the first remaining choice as your answer.

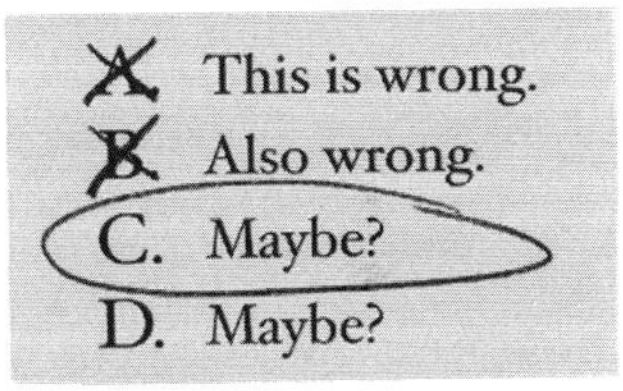

Whether you choose to select the first remaining choice, the second, or the last, the important thing is that you use some preselected standard. Using this approach guarantees that you will not be enticed into selecting an answer choice that looks right, because you are not basing your decision on how the answer choices look.

This is not meant to make you question your knowledge. Instead, it is to help you recognize the difference between your knowledge and your impressions. There's a huge difference between thinking an answer is right because of what you know, and thinking an answer is right because it looks or sounds like it should be right.

Summary: To ensure that your selection is appropriately random, make a predetermined selection from among all answer choices you have not eliminated.

Test-Taking Strategies

This section contains a list of test-taking strategies that you may find helpful as you work through the test. By taking what you know and applying logical thought, you can maximize your chances of answering any question correctly!

It is very important to realize that every question is different and every person is different: no single strategy will work on every question, and no single strategy will work for every person. That's why we've included all of them here, so you can try them out and determine which ones work best for different types of questions and which ones work best for you.

Question Strategies

✓ Read Carefully

Read the question and the answer choices carefully. Don't miss the question because you misread the terms. You have plenty of time to read each question thoroughly and make sure you understand what is being asked. Yet a happy medium must be attained, so don't waste too much time. You must read carefully and efficiently.

✓ Contextual Clues

Look for contextual clues. If the question includes a word you are not familiar with, look at the immediate context for some indication of what the word might mean. Contextual clues can often give you all the information you need to decipher the meaning of an unfamiliar word. Even if you can't determine the meaning, you may be able to narrow down the possibilities enough to make a solid guess at the answer to the question.

✓ Prefixes

If you're having trouble with a word in the question or answer choices, try dissecting it. Take advantage of every clue that the word might include. Prefixes can be a huge help. Usually, they allow you to determine a basic meaning. *Pre-* means before, *post-* means after, *pro-* is positive, *de-* is negative. From prefixes, you can get an idea of the general meaning of the word and try to put it into context.

✓ Hedge Words

Watch out for critical hedge words, such as *likely, may, can, often, almost, mostly, usually, generally, rarely,* and *sometimes.* Question writers insert these hedge phrases to cover every possibility. Often an answer choice will be wrong simply because it leaves no room for exception. Be on guard for answer choices that have definitive words such as *exactly* and *always.*

✓ Switchback Words

Stay alert for *switchbacks.* These are the words and phrases frequently used to alert you to shifts in thought. The most common switchback words are *but, although,* and *however.* Others include *nevertheless, on the other hand, even though, while, in spite of, despite,* and *regardless of.* Switchback words are important to catch because they can change the direction of the question or an answer choice.

☑ FACE VALUE

When in doubt, use common sense. Accept the situation in the problem at face value. Don't read too much into it. These problems will not require you to make wild assumptions. If you have to go beyond creativity and warp time or space in order to have an answer choice fit the question, then you should move on and consider the other answer choices. These are normal problems rooted in reality. The applicable relationship or explanation may not be readily apparent, but it is there for you to figure out. Use your common sense to interpret anything that isn't clear.

Answer Choice Strategies

☑ ANSWER SELECTION

The most thorough way to pick an answer choice is to identify and eliminate wrong answers until only one is left, then confirm it is the correct answer. Sometimes an answer choice may immediately seem right, but be careful. The test writers will usually put more than one reasonable answer choice on each question, so take a second to read all of them and make sure that the other choices are not equally obvious. As long as you have time left, it is better to read every answer choice than to pick the first one that looks right without checking the others.

☑ ANSWER CHOICE FAMILIES

An answer choice family consists of two (in rare cases, three) answer choices that are very similar in construction and cannot all be true at the same time. If you see two answer choices that are direct opposites or parallels, one of them is usually the correct answer. For instance, if one answer choice says that quantity *x* increases and another either says that quantity *x* decreases (opposite) or says that quantity *y* increases (parallel), then those answer choices would fall into the same family. An answer choice that doesn't match the construction of the answer choice family is more likely to be incorrect. Most questions will not have answer choice families, but when they do appear, you should be prepared to recognize them.

☑ ELIMINATE ANSWERS

Eliminate answer choices as soon as you realize they are wrong, but make sure you consider all possibilities. If you are eliminating answer choices and realize that the last one you are left with is also wrong, don't panic. Start over and consider each choice again. There may be something you missed the first time that you will realize on the second pass.

☑ AVOID FACT TRAPS

Don't be distracted by an answer choice that is factually true but doesn't answer the question. You are looking for the choice that answers the question. Stay focused on what the question is asking for so you don't accidentally pick an answer that is true but incorrect. Always go back to the question and make sure the answer choice you've selected actually answers the question and is not merely a true statement.

☑ EXTREME STATEMENTS

In general, you should avoid answers that put forth extreme actions as standard practice or proclaim controversial ideas as established fact. An answer choice that states the "process should be used in certain situations, if..." is much more likely to be correct than one that states the "process should be discontinued completely." The first is a calm rational statement and doesn't even make a definitive, uncompromising stance, using a hedge word *if* to provide wiggle room, whereas the second choice is far more extreme.

⊘ Benchmark

As you read through the answer choices and you come across one that seems to answer the question well, mentally select that answer choice. This is not your final answer, but it's the one that will help you evaluate the other answer choices. The one that you selected is your benchmark or standard for judging each of the other answer choices. Every other answer choice must be compared to your benchmark. That choice is correct until proven otherwise by another answer choice beating it. If you find a better answer, then that one becomes your new benchmark. Once you've decided that no other choice answers the question as well as your benchmark, you have your final answer.

⊘ Predict the Answer

Before you even start looking at the answer choices, it is often best to try to predict the answer. When you come up with the answer on your own, it is easier to avoid distractions and traps because you will know exactly what to look for. The right answer choice is unlikely to be word-for-word what you came up with, but it should be a close match. Even if you are confident that you have the right answer, you should still take the time to read each option before moving on.

General Strategies

⊘ Tough Questions

If you are stumped on a problem or it appears too hard or too difficult, don't waste time. Move on! Remember though, if you can quickly check for obviously incorrect answer choices, your chances of guessing correctly are greatly improved. Before you completely give up, at least try to knock out a couple of possible answers. Eliminate what you can and then guess at the remaining answer choices before moving on.

⊘ Check Your Work

Since you will probably not know every term listed and the answer to every question, it is important that you get credit for the ones that you do know. Don't miss any questions through careless mistakes. If at all possible, try to take a second to look back over your answer selection and make sure you've selected the correct answer choice and haven't made a costly careless mistake (such as marking an answer choice that you didn't mean to mark). This quick double check should more than pay for itself in caught mistakes for the time it costs.

⊘ Pace Yourself

It's easy to be overwhelmed when you're looking at a page full of questions; your mind is confused and full of random thoughts, and the clock is ticking down faster than you would like. Calm down and maintain the pace that you have set for yourself. Especially as you get down to the last few minutes of the test, don't let the small numbers on the clock make you panic. As long as you are on track by monitoring your pace, you are guaranteed to have time for each question.

⊘ Don't Rush

It is very easy to make errors when you are in a hurry. Maintaining a fast pace in answering questions is pointless if it makes you miss questions that you would have gotten right otherwise. Test writers like to include distracting information and wrong answers that seem right. Taking a little extra time to avoid careless mistakes can make all the difference in your test score. Find a pace that allows you to be confident in the answers that you select.

⊘ Keep Moving

Panicking will not help you pass the test, so do your best to stay calm and keep moving. Taking deep breaths and going through the answer elimination steps you practiced can help to break through a stress barrier and keep your pace.

Final Notes

The combination of a solid foundation of content knowledge and the confidence that comes from practicing your plan for applying that knowledge is the key to maximizing your performance on test day. As your foundation of content knowledge is built up and strengthened, you'll find that the strategies included in this chapter become more and more effective in helping you quickly sift through the distractions and traps of the test to isolate the correct answer.

Now that you're preparing to move forward into the test content chapters of this book, be sure to keep your goal in mind. As you read, think about how you will be able to apply this information on the test. If you've already seen sample questions for the test and you have an idea of the question format and style, try to come up with questions of your own that you can answer based on what you're reading. This will give you valuable practice applying your knowledge in the same ways you can expect to on test day.

Good luck and good studying!

Institutions and Policy Processes

United States Federal Government Executive Branch

Term of Appointment and Qualifications for US President

The **President of the United States** is elected for a term of four years. The President may serve for a maximum of two terms. In order to be the President of the United States of America, an individual must be a natural-born citizen of the United States. Candidates for the position of United States President must also be at least thirty-five years of age. Finally, in order to become President of the United States of America, an individual must have been a resident of the United States for at least fourteen years.

Powers of the President of the United States

The President of the US is the Head of the **Executive Branch**. The powers of the President are defined by the US Constitution, and include the power to act as **Commander in Chief of US Armed Forces**; as such, the President can authorize the use of troops without a declaration of war. To declare war, the President must receive approval from Congress. The President must also receive the consent of Congress when using the power to make treaties, appoint the heads of Executive Branch departments, and appoint ambassadors, Supreme Court judges, federal judges, and other officials. The President also has the power to receive foreign ambassadors and other representatives of foreign nations, to provide a yearly State of the Union Address, to recommend legislation, to convene and adjourn Congress, to ensure that laws are carried out, to fill administrative openings when Congress is in recess, and to issue reprieves and pardons for crimes against the United States.

Legislative Powers of the President

The President can **recommend legislation** to members of Congress, who can then introduce it as a bill. Only Congress can create legislation, but the President's approval of a bill is significant in determining whether it will pass. The President may sign a bill into law, veto a bill, or do nothing with it once it has passed Congress and been sent to the President for approval. If the President **signs a bill into law**, only the Supreme Court can then dismiss it by finding it unconstitutional. If a bill is **vetoed**, it is sent back to Congress without the President's signature, where Congress can override the veto with two-thirds approval. If the President does nothing with a bill, and Congress is in session ten business days following the receipt of the bill by the President, it becomes **law** without the President's signature; if Congress adjourns within ten business days, the bill dies, which is referred to as a **pocket veto**. The President can only veto a bill in its entirety.

Review Video: Executive Branch
Visit mometrix.com/academy and enter code: 210629

Secretary of Agriculture and the Department of Agriculture

The Secretary of Agriculture is a member of the President's Cabinet and is the head of the **Department of Agriculture**, which was established in 1862. The Department of Agriculture is responsible for efforts to maintain and increase agricultural profits, as well as efforts to foster international markets for United States agricultural products. One of the purposes of the Department of Agriculture is to aid in alleviating poverty, hunger, and malnutrition. Another goal of the Department of Agriculture is to improve agricultural production by aiding in the protection of natural resources. The Department of Agriculture is responsible for ensuring the quality and safety of food by the use of inspection and grading activities.

Presidential Impeachment

By definition, impeachment is the first step in the process of **removing an official from office** by a charge of crime or misconduct while in office. In the case of the President of the United States, if the **House of Representatives** believes that the President has committed criminal activity or engaged in misconduct while in office, specifically treason, bribery, and other high crimes and misdemeanors, the House can **impeach** the President by majority vote. After the House has impeached the President, the **Senate** examines the case and votes to convict the President or not. If two-thirds of the Senate votes to convict the President, he is removed from his position. The process of impeachment is overseen by the **Chief Justice of the Supreme Court**.

President's Budget

The **Budget and Accounting Act of 1921** requires the President to submit an annual document to Congress by the first Monday of February containing the proposed spending plan for the Federal Government in the upcoming fiscal year. The budget is essentially a set of goals with associated costs. The purpose of the budget is to provide a guide for Congress to use when determining how much money to spend, what to spend money on, and how to raise money to meet spending goals. The **Office of Management and Budget** helps the President with the annual spending plan. Federal appropriations must be approved by Congress. When Congress receives the spending plan, the House of Representatives establishes a **level of spending** for the Federal Government. Finally, Congress determines how this level of spending will be allocated for various Federal actions.

President's Cabinet

The President's Cabinet is comprised of the heads of the executive departments, who **advise** the President on issues related to their respective departments on a weekly basis. Members of the **Cabinet** include the Vice President, the Attorney General, and the Secretaries of Agriculture, Commerce, Defense, Education, Energy, Health and Human Services, Homeland Security, Housing and Urban Development, Interior, Labor, State, Transportation, Treasury, and Veterans Affairs. Department heads are appointed by the President and confirmed by a majority vote in the Senate. They remain in their positions for the length of the President's administration, and when a new administration begins, the heads of the executive departments are expected to leave their positions. The President can fire the head of an executive department without approval from Congress.

Secretary of State

The Secretary of State is a member of the President's Cabinet and is the head of the **Department of State**, which was established in 1789. The Department of State is responsible for advising the President on foreign policy, implementing foreign policy, and working on behalf of American interests internationally. The Department of State works with citizens of the United States, Congress, other departments and agencies within the United States government, and foreign governments. The Department of State is responsible for negotiating international treaties and agreements and representing the United States in international organizations, including the United Nations, and at international meetings.

Secretary of the Treasury and the Department of the Treasury

The Secretary of the Treasury is a member of the President's Cabinet and is the head of the **Department of the Treasury**, which was established in 1789. The Department of the Treasury is responsible for developing and recommending economic, financial, tax, and fiscal policies, acting as the US government's primary financial agent, enforcing laws, and producing coins and currency.

The **Secretary of the Treasury** is the President's key advisor on national and international **financial, economic, and tax policy**. The Secretary of the Treasury also assists with developing wide-ranging economic policies and handles public debt.

Secretary of Defense and the Department of Defense

The Secretary of Defense is a member of the President's Cabinet and is the head of the **Department of Defense**, which was established in 1947. The Department of Defense is responsible for protecting United States security by supplying **armed forces**. The armed forces of the United States are comprised of the Army, Navy, Marine Corps, and Air Force. The Reserve and National Guard also exist as part of the Department of Defense to assist in case of emergency. The Defense Department is also staffed by civilian employees. The **Secretary of Defense** is responsible for directing and overseeing the Department of Defense.

Attorney General and the Department of Justice

The Attorney General is a member of the President's Cabinet and is the head of the **Department of Justice**, which was established in 1870. The Department of Justice is responsible for providing legal counsel for the people of the United States. The Department of Justice consists of lawyers, investigators, and federal agents. The **Attorney General** is responsible for directing the Department of Justice, and in rare circumstances will represent the United States government in Supreme Court cases. The Attorney General also advises the President and the other heads of the executive departments on **legal matters**.

Secretary of the Interior and the Department of the Interior

The Secretary of the interior is a member of the President's Cabinet and is the head of the **Department of the Interior**, which was established in 1849. The Department of the Interior is responsible for protecting and ensuring access to the **natural and cultural resources** of the United States. The Department of the Interior is also responsible for ensuring that the United States upholds its responsibilities to Native American tribes. The Department of the Interior administers the public lands and minerals, national parks, national wildlife refuges, and western water resources of the United States. The employees of the Department of the Interior work on issues related to migratory wildlife conservation, historic preservation, endangered species, and the protection and restoration of lands that have undergone surface mining, mapping, and geological, hydrological, and biological sciences.

Secretary of Commerce and the Department of Commerce

The Secretary of Commerce is a member of the President's Cabinet and is the head of the **Department of Commerce**, which was established in 1903. The Department of Commerce is responsible for furthering international trade, economic growth, and technological advancement opportunities for the United States. The Department of Commerce works to increase the competitiveness of the United States in the international economy and decrease unfair competition in international trade. The Department of Commerce also conducts social and economic statistical analysis; conducts science, engineering, and technology research; and makes efforts to advance knowledge and utilization of the physical environment and ocean resources. In addition, the Department of Commerce issues patents and trademarks. The Department of Commerce also researches and makes policies related to telecommunications, aids in fostering domestic economic growth, and works to further the development of minority-owned businesses.

The **Secretary of Commerce** advises the President on issues pertaining to the **industrial and commercial areas** of the United States economy.

Secretary of Labor and the Department of Labor

The Secretary of Labor is a member of the President's Cabinet and is the head of the **Department of Labor**, which was established in 1913. The Department of Labor is responsible for advancing the well-being of workers in the United States, bettering working conditions, and increasing the employment opportunities available to workers. To meet these responsibilities, the Department of Labor administers **Federal labor laws** to ensure the rights of employees to a safe working environment, a minimum wage, overtime pay, unemployment insurance, and workers' compensation. The Department of Labor also administers labor laws to ensure that discrimination does not occur in the workplace. Other efforts that the Department of Labor makes in the interest of workers involve the protection of employee pension rights, job training programs, job placement programs, improving collective bargaining ability, and monitoring economic indicators related to employment.

Secretary and Department of Health and Human Services

The Secretary of Health and Human Services is a member of the President's Cabinet and is the head of the **Department of Health and Human Services**, which was established in 1953. The Department of Health and Human Services is responsible for protecting the health of the citizens of the United States and providing vital human services. The Department of Health and Human Services conducts health and social science research, conducts research aimed at preventing disease, researches and provides immunization services, works to ensure food and drug safety, manages Medicare and Medicaid, provides health information technology, provides financial aid and services for low-income families, works to better maternal and infant health, manages the program Head Start for pre-school students, supports community programs, works to reduce child abuse and domestic violence, supports substance abuse treatment and prevention, supports services for the elderly, ensures health services for Native Americans, and prepares for medical emergencies. The **Secretary of Health and Human Services** provides advice to the President on issues regarding **health, welfare, and income security**.

Housing and Urban Development and the Department of Housing

The Secretary of Housing and Urban Development is a member of the President's Cabinet and is the head of the **Department of Housing and Urban Development**, which was established in 1965. The Department of Housing and Urban Development is responsible for developing programs and policies related to **housing and community development** in the United States. Specifically, the Department of Housing and Urban Development administers housing assistance programs, fosters state and local involvement in addressing housing and community development issues, and promotes donations from private house building and mortgage lending companies to housing and community development programs.

Secretary of Transportation and the Department of Transportation

The Secretary of Transportation is a member of the President's Cabinet and is the head of the **Department of Transportation**, which was established in 1966. The Department of Transportation is responsible for developing **transportation policy** in the United States, including with relation to highway planning, development, and construction, mass transportation in urban areas, railroads, aviation, and the safety and security of the waterways, ports, highways, and oil and gas pipelines of the United States. The Department of Transportation develops transportation policy in coordination with state and local agencies and organizations. Transportation policies greatly impact other sectors, including land management, resource conservation, and technology.

Secretary of Energy and the Department of Energy

The Secretary of Energy is a member of the President's Cabinet and is the head of the **Department of Energy**, which was established in 1977. The Department of Energy is responsible for developing and sharing technical, scientific, and educational information with leaders and policy-makers in order to foster efficient energy consumption, the development and implementation of a wide variety of energy sources, economic production and competition, higher standards of environmental quality, and a secure and stable defense program for the United States.

Secretary of Education and the Department of Education

The Secretary of Education is a member of the President's Cabinet and is the head of the **Department of Education**, which was established in 1979. The Department of Education is responsible for developing policies and administering federal assistance for **educational programs**. The goal of the Department of Education is to provide equal access to education for all citizens of the United States and to foster quality educational programs. The Secretary of Education provides advice to the President related to education policies and programs.

Secretary of Veterans Affairs and the Department of Veterans Affairs

The Secretary of Veterans Affairs is a member of the President's Cabinet and is the head of the **Department of Veterans Affairs**, which was established in 1988. The Department of Veterans Affairs is responsible for administering programs with the goal of providing benefits to veterans and their families. Specifically, the Department of Veterans Affairs provides funds for disabilities or death that results from military service, pensions, educational benefits, rehabilitation benefits, home loan guaranties, burial benefits, and a healthcare program that encompasses nursing homes, clinics, and medical centers for veterans. The Department of Veterans Affairs is made up of the **Veterans Health Administration**, the **Veterans Benefits Administration**, and the **National Cemetery Administration**, each of which has a central office and field offices.

Secretary of Homeland Security and the Department of Homeland Security

The Secretary of Homeland Security is a member of the President's Cabinet and is the head of the **Department of Homeland Security**, which was established in 2003. The Department of Homeland Security is responsible for efforts aimed at preventing **terrorist attacks** against the United States. The Department of Homeland Security is also responsible for efforts to reduce the susceptibility of the United States to terrorism. In addition, the Department of Homeland Security is responsible for efforts aimed at reducing the devastation and suffering from potential terrorist attacks and natural disasters.

Presidential Succession Act of 1947

The Presidential Succession Act of 1947 specifies the order of **succession** if the President of the United States is unable to carry out the duties and responsibilities of the office of the President due to death, resignation, removal from office, or due to conditions that otherwise render the President incapacitated. In such a situation, the office of the President will be filled by the following people, in order: Vice President, Speaker of the House, President Pro Tempore of the Senate, Secretary of State, Secretary of the Treasury, Secretary of Defense, Attorney General, Secretary of the Interior, Secretary of Agriculture, Secretary of Commerce, Secretary of Labor, Secretary of Health and Human Services, Secretary of Housing and Urban Development, Secretary of Transportation, Secretary of Energy, Secretary of Education, Secretary of Veterans Affairs, and finally Secretary of Homeland Security.

United States Federal Government Legislative Branch

Congress

Congress represents one part of the legislative branch in the United States. **Congress** is composed of two chambers known as the **House of Representatives** and the **Senate**. The two-chamber system is referred to as a **bicameral legislative system**. Congress is responsible for writing, debating, and passing **bills**. Once bills are passed by Congress, they go to the President of the United States to be reviewed, approved, and signed into law. Congress is also responsible for investigating issues that are important on a national level and for overseeing both the executive and judicial branches. Elections are held every two years for all 435 members of the House of Representatives and for one-third of the members of the Senate. Congress begins a new session every January after Congressional elections. Congress convenes once a year, typically from January 3rd through July 31st.

Powers of Congress

Article I, Section 8 of the Constitution gives Congress the power to establish and collect taxes, to pay debts, to provide for the defense of the country, to borrow money on credit, to regulate domestic and international commerce, to establish immigration policy, to establish bankruptcies laws, to create money, to establish a postal system, to protect patents and intellectual property rights, to create lower courts, to control and protect citizens and ships in international waters, to declare war, to establish and maintain an army and a navy, to maintain National Guard readiness, and to exercise control over the District of Columbia and other federal property. Section 8 also includes a clause known as the **Elastic Clause**, which gives Congress the power to pass any law necessary for carrying out the actions over which it has power.

Legislative Branch

The Legislative branch was established by **Article I** of the United States Constitution. The **Legislative branch** is responsible for making laws. In the United States, the Legislative branch is a **bicameral system**, which means that it is divided into two houses, the **House of Representatives** and the **Senate**. The bicameral system ensures that **checks and balances** exist within the Legislative branch. Representatives and Senators are elected by the people in the state that they represent. Also included in the Legislative branch are all of the agencies that provide support to Congress, including the Government Printing Office, the Library of Congress, the Congressional Budget Office, the General Accounting Office, and the Architect of the Capitol.

Review Video: Legislative Branch
Visit mometrix.com/academy and enter code: 405303

Review Video: Bicameral Legislature
Visit mometrix.com/academy and enter code: 756921

Committee System

The Congressional committee system started in 1789. **Congressional committees** are created to address political, social, and economic changes. Both the House and the Senate have their own committees, and there are also **joint committees** between both houses. To address an increasing number of issues that must be discussed, **subcommittees** have also formed. Committees are responsible for investigating each bill that is proposed to Congress. This investigation could include holding hearings where expert witnesses provide information and facts that are relevant to the bill. Once the committee has heard all the facts, it either recommends the bill as it was originally written or it suggests that the bill should be passed with amendments. Occasionally, bills are **tabled**, or put aside, which stops consideration of those bills. Once a bill is passed in each house, a committee called the conference committee works to find common ground between House and Senate versions of the bill. After both houses agree to the same version of the bill and it passes a final vote, it is sent to the President.

House of Representatives

There are 435 members of the **House of Representatives**. Every member represents a region within a state; these regions are referred to as congressional districts and are based on population size. Congressional districts are established every ten years through the process of a **population census,** which is carried out by the US Census Bureau. The number of congressional districts in a state determines how many Representatives are from that state. Every state has at least one seat in the House. Representatives come not only from the fifty states but, in addition, five members represent Puerto Rico, Guam, American Samoa, the Virgin Islands, and D.C. These five members are not permitted to vote in Congress but are permitted to engage in debates. The House is solely responsible for initiating laws that require citizens to pay taxes and for determining whether government officials should be tried for committing crimes against the US.

Standing Committees of the House of Representatives

Although Congressional committees are created to address changing political, social, and economic conditions, there are a number of committees that are permanent, known as **standing committees**. The standing committees within the **House of Representatives** include the Agriculture Committee, the Appropriations Committee, the Armed Services Committee, the Banking and Financial Services Committee, the Budget Committee, the Commerce Committee, the Education and the Workforce Committee, the Government Reform and Oversight Committee, the House Administration Committee, the International Relations Committee, the Judiciary Committee, the Resources Committee, the Rules Committee, the Science Committee, the Small Business Committee, the Standards of Official Conduct Committee, the Transportation and Infrastructure Committee, the Veterans' Affairs Committee, and the Ways and Means Committee.

House Committee on Agriculture

The House Committee on Agriculture was established in 1820. The committee has jurisdiction over the degradation of seeds, over the control of insect pests, and over the protection of fauna in forest reserves. The committee also has jurisdiction over agriculture, agricultural and industrial chemistry, agricultural colleges and laboratories, agricultural economics, agricultural education extension services, agricultural production and marketing, prices of agricultural products and commodities, animal industries, animal disease, commodity exchanges, crop insurance, soil conservation, the dairy industry, entomology, plant quarantine, extension of farm credit and farm security, inspection of meat and seafood products, forestry, human nutrition and home economics, plant industry, soils, agricultural engineering, rural electrification, rural development, and water conservation. Subcommittees include the Subcommittee on Conservation, Credit, Rural Development and Research; the Subcommittee on General Farm Commodities and Risk Management; the Subcommittee on Specialty Crops and Foreign Agriculture Programs; the Subcommittee on Department Operations, Oversight, Dairy, Nutrition and Forestry; and the Subcommittee on Livestock and Horticulture.

House Committee on Appropriations

The House Committee on Appropriations was created in 1865. The committee has jurisdiction over the appropriation of money to government departments, the withdrawal of appropriations, and the transfer of unspent funds. The committee holds hearings to review budget recommendations and policies of the President and to review the financial factors used to come up with the budget.

Subcommittees of the House Committee on Appropriations include the Subcommittee on Agriculture, Rural Development, Food and Drug Administration, and Related Agencies; the Subcommittee on Defense; the Subcommittee on Energy and Water Development, and Related Agencies; the Subcommittee on Foreign Operations, Export Financing and Related Programs; the Subcommittee on Homeland Security; the Subcommittee on Interior, Environment, and Related Agencies; the Subcommittee on Labor, Health and Human Services, Education, and Related Agencies; the Subcommittee on Military Quality of Life and Veterans Affairs, and Related Agencies; the Subcommittee on Science, the Departments of State, Justice, and Commerce, and Related Agencies; and the Subcommittee on Transportation, Treasury, and Housing and Urban Development, The Judiciary, and District of Columbia.

House Committee on Armed Services

The House Committee on Armed Services has jurisdiction over matters related to defense and the Department of Defense, including the Departments of the Army, Navy and Air Force, ammunition storage facilities, forts, arsenals, and Army, Navy, and Air Force locations. In addition, the committee has jurisdiction over the conservation, cultivation, and use of naval oil reserves, as well as canals connecting oceans, the Merchant Marine Academy, and state Merchant Marine Academies. The committee also has jurisdiction over nuclear energy as it is applied within the military, tactical intelligence, matters related to the merchant marine that affect national security, the salaries and benefits of individuals who are in the armed forces, scientific R&D for the armed forces, the selective service, the size and makeup of the armed forces, soldiers and sailors homes, and materials required to provide defense. Subcommittees include the Tactical Air and Land Forces Subcommittee; the Readiness Subcommittee; the Terrorism, Unconventional Threats and Capabilities Subcommittee; the Military Personnel Subcommittee; the Strategic Forces Subcommittee; and the Projection Forces Subcommittee.

House Committee on the Budget

The House Committee on the Budget is responsible for developing a budget resolution that establishes spending and revenue levels for federal programs. The committee has oversight over the laws and regulations that are relevant to the **budget process**, as well as over the agencies that hold the responsibility for the administration of such laws. Specifically, the committee has jurisdiction over the Budget and Accounting Act of 1920, the Congressional Budget Act of 1974, and the Emergency Balanced Budget and Deficit Control Act of 1985, and the agencies over which it holds jurisdiction include the Office of Management and Budget and the Congressional Budget Office. The committee also investigates tax expenditures and the impact of legislation on budget expenditures. In addition, the committee has jurisdiction over budget priorities, budget enforcement, budget process reform, and direct spending and tax incentives.

House Committee on Education and the Workforce: Education

The House Committee on Education and the Workforce was created in 1997. The committee has jurisdiction over issues concerning education and labor. All levels of **education** are addressed by the committee, including elementary and secondary education programs, the Every Student Succeeds Act, school choice for low-income individuals, special education, educator quality and educator training, scientific reading instruction, vocational and technical education, higher education programs, college access for low and middle-income individuals, financial aid, early childhood and preschool programs, Head Start, school lunch and nutrition, financial oversight of the US Department of Education, care and treatment of at-risk children, child abuse prevention, child adoption, educational research and advancement, adult education, and anti-poverty programs.

HOUSE COMMITTEE ON EDUCATION AND THE WORKFORCE: WORKFORCE

The House Committee on Education and the Workforce was created in 1997. The committee has jurisdiction over issues concerning education and labor. The committee promotes efforts to improve health care, job training, and retirement security for **workers**. The committee also promotes efforts to advance opportunities for people, especially in the area of emerging knowledge. Specific items on the agenda of the committee with regard to workforce include pension and retirement security for workers, access to health care and other benefits for workers, job training, adult education, and workforce development, welfare reform, protecting democratic rights for union members, health and safety, offering more scheduling and work arrangement choices and flexibility for workers, equal employment opportunity, civil rights, wages and hours of labor, workers' compensation, family and medical leave, the relationships between employers and employees.

HOUSE COMMITTEE ON ENERGY AND COMMERCE

The House Committee on Energy and Commerce is the longest-standing committee in the House of Representatives. The committee has broad jurisdiction, including jurisdiction over issues pertaining to telecommunications, consumer protection, food and drug safety, public health, air quality, environmental health, supply and delivery of energy, and interstate and foreign commerce. The committee has jurisdiction over the Department of Energy, the Department of Health and Human Services, the Department of Transportation, the Federal Trade Commission, the Food and Drug Administration, and the Federal Communications Commission. Subcommittees of the House Committee on Energy and Commerce include the Subcommittee on Commerce, Trade and Consumer Protection; the Subcommittee on Energy and Air Quality; the Subcommittee on Environment and Hazardous Materials; the Subcommittee on Health; the Subcommittee on Oversight and Investigations; and the Subcommittee on Telecommunications and the Internet.

HOUSE COMMITTEE ON FINANCIAL SERVICES

The House Committee on Financial Services has jurisdiction over banks and banking, stabilization of the economy, defense production, commodity, rent, service prices, financial assistance for commerce and industry, insurance, international finance, international financial and monetary organizations, money and credit, public and private housing, securities and exchanges, and urban development. The House Committee on Financial Services has several subcommittees, including the Subcommittee on Capital Markets, Insurance, and Government Sponsored Enterprises; the Subcommittee on Domestic and International Monetary Policy, Trade, and Technology; the Subcommittee on Financial Institutions and Consumer Credit; the Subcommittee on Housing and Community Opportunity; and the Subcommittee on Oversight and Investigations.

HOUSE COMMITTEE ON GOVERNMENT REFORM

The House Committee on Government Reform is the most important legislative **investigative and oversight committee**. The committee has oversight over the National Guard, the Reserves, Homeland Security, the US Postal Service, management reform, diploma mills, electronic voting, regulatory affairs, the Bureau of Economic Analysis, the Unfunded Mandates Reform Act, new dietary guidelines, the thrift savings plan, security clearance reform, federal agency contracting, the General Services Administration, information technology and information policy, intellectual property piracy, the Department of the interior's tribal recognition process, D.C., flu vaccine supply and state and local health preparedness, FDA post-marketing surveillance, USDA cattle surveillance, and 21st-century healthcare. There are numerous subcommittees of the House Committee on Government Reform, including the Subcommittee on Criminal Justice, Drug Policy and Human Resources; the Subcommittee on Energy and Resources; the Subcommittee on Federalism and the Census; the Subcommittee on Federal Workforce and Agency Organization; the Subcommittee on

Government Management, Finance, and Accountability; the Subcommittee on National Security, Emerging Threats, and International Relations; and the Subcommittee on Regulatory Affairs.

House Committee on Homeland Security

The House Committee on Homeland Security has jurisdiction over a wide spectrum of issues and factors pertaining to the prevention of **terrorist attacks** on the US, particularly involving weapons that are characterized as nuclear and biological weapons. The subcommittees of the Committee on Homeland Security include the Subcommittee on Prevention of Nuclear and Biological Attack; the Subcommittee on Intelligence, Information Sharing, and Terrorism Risk Assessment; the Subcommittee on Economic Security, Infrastructure Protection, and Cybersecurity; the Subcommittee on Management, Integration, and Oversight; the Subcommittee on Emergency Preparedness, Science, and Technology; and the Subcommittee on Investigations.

House Committee on House Administration

The House Committee on House Administration is responsible for overseeing **federal elections** as well as the daily functions of the **House of Representatives**. Specifically, the Committee on House Administration has jurisdiction over the Library of Congress, statues and pictures, the acceptance of or purchase of works of art for the Capitol, and the Botanic Garden. The **Committee on House Administration** also has jurisdiction over the purchase of books and manuscripts and the Smithsonian Institution. The Committee on House Administration is also responsible for the oversight of the establishment of other institutions similar to the Smithsonian Institution.

House Committee on International Relations

The House Committee on International Relations has jurisdiction over issues pertaining to international relations between the US and other countries, procurement of property for US embassies, the delineation of boundaries between the US and other countries, export controls, nonproliferation of nuclear technology, foreign loans, international commodity agreements, international conferences and congresses, international education, international intervention and war, diplomacy, efforts to promote US commercial interests globally, international economic policy, neutrality, protection of US citizens abroad, the American Red Cross, trading with enemies, and the United Nations. Subcommittees of the House Committee on International Relations include the Subcommittee on Asia and the Pacific; the Subcommittee on Africa, Global Human Rights, and International Operations; the Subcommittee on the Western Hemisphere; the Subcommittee on Europe and Emerging Threats; the Subcommittee on the Middle East and Central Asia; the Subcommittee on Oversight and Investigations; and the Subcommittee on International Terrorism and Nonproliferation.

House Committee on the Judiciary

The House Committee on the Judiciary was created in 1813. The committee has jurisdiction over the judiciary, both civil and criminal judicial proceedings, administrative practices and procedures, the apportionment of Representatives, bankruptcy, mutiny, espionage, counterfeiting, civil liberties, constitutional amendments, criminal law enforcement, federal courts and judges, local courts in US territories and possessions, immigration policy, interstate compacts, cases against the US government, members of Congress, national jails, patents, the Patent and Trademark Office, copyrights, trademarks, succession to the office of President, protection of trade and commerce against illegal obstacles and monopolies, revision and codification of statutes, the boundaries of states and territories, and activities that are considered treacherous and threatening to the security of the US. Subcommittees include the Subcommittee on Courts, the Internet, and Intellectual Property; the Subcommittee on Immigration, Border Security, and Claims; the Subcommittee on

Commercial and Administrative Law; the Subcommittee on Crime, Terrorism, and Homeland Security; and the Subcommittee on the Constitution.

HOUSE COMMITTEE ON RESOURCES

The House Committee on Resources has jurisdiction over issues pertaining to fisheries and wildlife, forest reserves and national parks, forfeiture of land grants and alien ownership, the Geological Survey, international fishing agreements, irrigation, interstate compacts related to the allocation of water for irrigation, reclamation, Native Americans, insular possessions of the US, military parks, battlefields, national cemeteries, the establishment of monuments and memorials, mineral land laws and claims, mineral resources on public land, mining interests, mining schools and laboratories, marine affairs, oceanography, petroleum conservation on public lands, preservation of prehistoric ruins, public lands, US government relations with Native Americans and Native American tribes, and the trans-Alaska oil pipeline. Subcommittees include the Subcommittee on Energy and Mineral Resources; the Subcommittee on Fisheries and Oceans; the Subcommittee on Forests and Forest Health; the Subcommittee on National Parks; and the Subcommittee on Water and Power.

HOUSE COMMITTEE ON RULES

The House Committee on Rules has two subcommittees. The first subcommittee is the **Subcommittee on the Rules and Organization of the House**. This subcommittee has responsibilities concerning issues regarding the relationship between the House of Representatives and the Senate, as well as issues regarding the relationship between Congress and the Judicial Branch. The Subcommittee on the Rules and Organization of the House also has responsibilities related to the internal operations of the House of Representatives. The second subcommittee is the **Subcommittee on the Legislative and Budget Process**. This subcommittee has responsibilities concerning issues regarding the relationship between Congress and the Executive Branch. The Subcommittee on the Legislative and Budget Process also has responsibilities related to the Congressional budget process.

HOUSE COMMITTEE ON SCIENCE

The House Committee on Science has jurisdiction over issues pertaining to all federal scientific research and development that is not military related. The committee has jurisdiction over the National Aeronautics and Space Administration, the Department of Energy, the Environmental Protection Agency, the National Science Foundation, the Federal Aviation Administration, the National Oceanic and Atmospheric Administration, the National Institute of Standards and Technology, the Federal Emergency Management Agency, the US Fire Administration, and the US Geological Survey. Subcommittees of the House Committee on Science include the Subcommittee on Environment, Technology, and Standards, the Subcommittee on Energy, the Subcommittee on Research, and the Subcommittee on Space and Aeronautics.

HOUSE COMMITTEE ON SMALL BUSINESS

The House Committee on Small Business has jurisdiction over issues pertaining to the Small Business Administration, financial and management programs and technical assistance programs for small businesses, advocacy for small businesses, issues related to veterans and small businesses, technology and research assistance programs for small businesses, the Small Business Technology Transfer program, federal procurement, government competition and regulatory flexibility, paperwork reduction, government regulation, taxation, energy, the Government Performance and Results Act, empowerment for small businesses in high-risk areas, workforce issues, health care, pensions, e-commerce, telecommunications, international trade, self-employment, manufacturing, agricultural and rural matters, and review of relevant regulations. The subcommittees of the House

Committee on Small Business include the Subcommittee on Workforce, Empowerment, and Government Programs; the Subcommittee on Regulatory Reform and Oversight; the Subcommittee on Tax, Finance, and Exports; and the Subcommittee on Rural Enterprises, Agriculture, and Technology.

House Committee on Standards of Official Conduct

The House Committee on Standards of Official Conduct implements the **ethics program** for the House of Representatives, as each branch of the federal government has the responsibility of implementing its own ethics program. Each house of the legislative branch has its own ethics committee to implement its ethics program; the counterpart to the House Committee on Standards of Official Conduct is the Senate Select Committee on Ethics. The House Committee on Standards of Official Conduct has jurisdiction over issues pertaining to the **House Code of Official Conduct**. The committee has jurisdiction to create or administer standards of official conduct; to investigate violations of the code of official conduct, laws, and regulations; to provide reports to government authorities of evidence of violations of laws; to give opinions about the appropriateness of the conduct of individuals associated with the House of Representatives; and to review requests for exceptions to the gift rule, and has jurisdiction over the Ethics in Government Act and the Foreign Gifts the Decorations Act.

House Committee on Transportation and Infrastructure

The House Committee on Transportation and Infrastructure has jurisdiction over issues pertaining to aviation, the Coast Guard and maritime transportation, economic development, public buildings, emergency management, highways, public transit, pipelines, railways, and water resources and environmental issues. The subcommittees of the House Committee on Transportation and Infrastructure include the Subcommittee on Aviation; the Subcommittee on the Coast Guard and Maritime Transportation; the Subcommittee on Economic Development, Public Buildings and Emergency Management; the Subcommittee on Highways, Transit, and Pipelines; the Subcommittee on Railroads; and the Subcommittee on Water Resources and Environment.

House Committee on Veterans' Affairs

The House Committee on Veterans' Affairs has jurisdiction over issues pertaining to **veterans** in a broad sense. The committee also has jurisdiction over pensions for veterans of all wars and over life insurance provided by the federal government for veterans of the armed services. In addition, the House Committee on Veterans' Affairs has jurisdiction over issues pertaining to the compensation of veterans and over vocational training and educational programs for veterans. The committee also has jurisdiction over veterans hospitals, medical services for veterans, civil relief for sailors and soldiers, services that assist individuals who have served in the armed forces in acclimating from life in the armed forces back into civilian life, and national cemeteries. The committee has specific jurisdiction over the Department of Veterans Affairs. Subcommittees include the Subcommittee on Disability Assistance and Memorial Affairs, the Subcommittee on Economic Opportunity, the Subcommittee on Health, and the Subcommittee on Oversight and Investigations.

House Committee on Ways and Means

The House Committee on Ways and Means has jurisdiction over customs, collection districts, ports, reciprocal trade agreements, broad efforts to generate revenue, efforts to generate revenue that are specifically associated with US insular possessions, US government debt, deposit of public funds, duties on goods, organizations that are exempt from paying taxes, and social security. Subcommittees of the House Committee on Ways and Means include the Subcommittee on Trade, the Subcommittee on Oversight, the Subcommittee on Health, the Subcommittee on Social Security, the Subcommittee on Human Resources, and the Subcommittee on Select Revenue Measures.

House Permanent Select Committee on Intelligence

The House Permanent Select Committee on Intelligence has the responsibility for overseeing many government organizations and their activities, including the Central Intelligence Agency, the Defense Intelligence Agency, the Department of Defense, the Department of Energy, the Department of Homeland Security, the Department of Justice, the Department of State, the Department of Treasury, the Federal Bureau of Investigation, the National Geospatial-Intelligence Agency, the National Reconnaissance Office, the National Security Agency, the Office of Naval Intelligence, the US Air Force Intelligence, Surveillance, and Reconnaissance, the US Army Intelligence and Security Command, the US Coast Guard, and the US Marine Corps Intelligence Department. Subcommittees of the House Permanent Select Committee on Intelligence include the Subcommittee on Terrorism/HUMINT, Analysis, and Counterintelligence, the Subcommittee on Technical and Tactical Intelligence, the Subcommittee on Intelligence Policy, and the Subcommittee on Oversight.

Election Process and Powers of the House of Representatives

Members of the House of Representatives are elected for **two-year terms**. Each state has at least one Representative, and the number of Representatives in each state depends upon its **population** as reported in the most recent census. Each state is divided into **congressional districts**. There is a Representative for every congressional district, who is elected by the voters in that district. There are 435 members of the House of Representatives, and Congress has the power to alter the total membership. A Representative must be at least 25 years old, a citizen of the United States for at least seven years, and a resident of the state to which they are elected. The House of Representatives has the power of impeachment.

Senate

There are 100 members of the **United States Senate**. The US Constitution stipulates that the **Vice President** of the United States controls the Senate and is therefore referred to as the president of the Senate. However, in reality, the Vice President is not regularly in attendance when the Senate is in session; rather, the Vice President is typically only in attendance during significant ceremonial events and when he is required to vote to break a tie within the Senate. The Senate is solely responsible for either confirming or disapproving of **treaties** that are drafted by the United States President. The Senate is also solely responsible for either confirming or disapproving of **appointments** made by the United States President, including Cabinet-level appointments, officers, Supreme Court judges, and ambassadors. In addition, the Senate is solely responsible for **trying government officials** who commit crimes against the United States.

Standing Committees of the Senate

Although Congressional committees are created to address changing political, social, and economic conditions, there are a number of committees that are permanent, known as **standing committees**. The standing committees within the Senate include the Agriculture, Nutrition, and Forestry Committee; the Appropriations Committee; the Armed Services Committee; the Banking Committee; the Budget Committee; the Commerce, Science, and Transportation Committee; the Energy and Natural Resources Committee; the Environment and Public Works Committee; the Finance Committee; the Foreign Relations Committee; the Governmental Affairs Committee; the Health, Education, Labor, and Pension Committee; the Indian Affairs Committee; the Judiciary Committee; the Rules and Administration Committee; the Small Business Committee; and the Veterans' Affairs Committee.

Senate Standing Committee on Agriculture, Nutrition, and Forestry

The Standing Committee on Agriculture, Nutrition, and Forestry was created in the year 1825. The committee writes legislation that addresses nutrition and food programs, the promotion of United

States agricultural products in global markets, the development of rural areas, agricultural research, and conservation programs. The main legislation associated with the committee is known as the Farm Bill. Subcommittees of the Senate Standing Committee on Agriculture, Nutrition, and Forestry include the Subcommittee on Production and Price Competitiveness; the Subcommittee on Forestry, Conservation, and Rural Revitalization; and the Subcommittee on Research, Nutrition, and General Legislation.

Senate Standing Committee on Appropriations

The Senate Standing Committee on Appropriations was created in 1867. The committee is the biggest in the US Senate. It is responsible for **appropriating funds** before money from the US treasury can be spent. The committee allocates money to government agencies, departments, and organizations every year. Appropriations may not exceed the budget limits established by the Senate Budget Committee. There are twelve subcommittees of the Appropriations Committee that review the President's budget requests, listen to expert testimonies, and draft spending plans. Subcommittees pass information they gather to the Senate Appropriations Committee, which can review and change spending bills before passing them to the Senate to be considered. Subcommittees include Agriculture, Rural Development, and Related Agencies; Commerce, Justice, and Science; Defense; District of Columbia; Energy and Water; Homeland Security; Interior and Related Agencies; Labor, Health, and Human Services; Education and Related Agencies; Legislative Branch; Military Construction and Veterans Affairs; State, Foreign Operations, and Related Programs; Transportation; Treasury; the Judiciary; and Housing and Urban Development and Related Agencies.

Senate Standing Committee on Armed Services

The Senate Standing Committee on Armed Services is concerned with aeronautical and space matters associated with military operations and weapons development; defense; the Department of Defense, the Department of the Army, the Department of the Navy, and the Department of the Air Force; the Panama Canal; research and development associated with and carried out by the military; nuclear energy issues that are related to national security; naval petroleum reserves outside of Alaska; salaries and benefits for military personnel and their families; the selective service; and materials needed for defense. The committee is also responsible for investigating issues pertaining to defense policy in the US. Beneath the full committee are the Subcommittee on Airland, the Subcommittee on Emerging Threats and Capabilities, the Subcommittee on Personnel, the Subcommittee on Readiness and Management Support, the Subcommittee on Seapower, and the Subcommittee on Strategic Forces.

Senate Standing Committee on Banking, Housing, and Urban Affairs

The Senate Standing Committee on Banking, Housing, and Urban Affairs is concerned with financial institutions, price control for commodities, rents and services, deposit insurance, maintaining a stable economy and keeping up defense production, promoting exports and stimulating foreign trade, establishing export controls, federal monetary policy, financial assistance for commerce and industry, issuing and redeeming notes, money and credit, the building of nursing homes, public and private housing, renegotiation of Government contracts, urban development, and public transportation. Beneath the full committee are the Subcommittee on Securities and Investment, the Subcommittee on Financial Institutions, the Subcommittee on Housing and Transportation, the Subcommittee on Economic Policy, and the Subcommittee on International Trade and Finance.

Senate Standing Committee on Budget

The Senate Standing Committee on the Budget was created in 1974. The Senate Standing Committee on the Budget has the responsibility for writing the **annual Congressional budget plan** and also for tracking actions related to the federal budget. The jurisdiction of the Senate Standing Committee on the Budget extends to oversight of the operation of the Congressional Budget Office. The purpose of the Senate Standing Committee on the Budget preparing the budget plan, also referred to as the budget resolution, is to lay out a general map for Congress with regard to the levels of government revenues and expenditures that are possible for the entire government. However, other Congressional Committees also draft legislation, and this legislation drafted by other committees is the legislation that enacts policies related to government spending and taxing.

Senate Standing Committee on Commerce, Science, and Transportation

There have been many predecessors to the Senate Standing Committee on Commerce, Science, and Transportation. The committee as it exists and is named today was previously known simply as the Committee on Commerce; the name was changed to its current name in 1977. Along with the change in name, the scope of the committee's jurisdiction was expanded. The standing committee and its subcommittees deal with the Coast Guard, coastal zone management, communications, highway safety, inland waterways, and interstate commerce. In addition, the committee addresses marine and ocean navigation, safety, and transportation; deepwater ports; marine fisheries; merchant marine and navigation; aeronautical and space sciences that are not military in nature; oceans; weather; and atmospheric activities; the Panama Canal and other canals that connect oceans; regulation of consumer products and services; regulation of interstate transportation; science; engineering; and technology R&D and policy; sports; standards and measurement; transportation; and transportation and commerce aspects of Outer Continental Shelf lands.

Senate Standing Committee on Energy and Natural Resources

The Committee on Energy and Natural Resources is the successor of the Committee on Public Lands, a very old Congressional committee, and therefore the jurisdiction of the committee has existed for nearly two hundred years. The name was changed from the Committee on Public Lands to the **Committee on Energy and Natural Resources** in 1977. The full committee has jurisdiction over energy policy, nuclear waste policy, privatization of federal government assets, territorial policy, issues pertaining to Native Hawaiian concerns, and ad hoc matters that include those which necessitate an expedited process, those which overlap the specialties of multiple subcommittees, and those which hold national importance. The Committee on Energy and Natural Resources has several subcommittees, including the Subcommittee on Energy, the Subcommittee on National Parks, the Subcommittee on Public Lands and Forests, and the Subcommittee on Water and Power.

Senate Standing Committee on Environment and Public Works

The full Senate Standing Committee on Environment and Public Works has the responsibility for overseeing issues pertaining to biotechnology, the Council on Environmental Quality, Earth Day, the Convention on International Trade in Endangered Species, environmental conflict resolution, environmental education, environmental justice, the Environmental Protection Agency, environmental treaties, the Morris K. Udall Foundation for Scholarship and Excellence in National Environmental Policy, the National Environmental Education Act of 1969, the Noise Control Act of 1972, noise pollution, and nominations. There are a number of subcommittees of the Senate Standing Committee on Environment and Public Works, including the Subcommittee on Transportation and Infrastructure; the Subcommittee on Clean Air, Climate Change, and Nuclear Safety; the Subcommittee on Fish, Wildlife, and Water; and the Subcommittee on Superfund and Waste Management.

Senate Standing Committee on Finance

The Senate Standing Committee on Finance has jurisdiction over issues pertaining to the debts of the United States, customs, collection districts, ports, deposit of public money, general revenue sharing, health programs of the Social Security Act or funded by special taxes or trust funds, social security, reciprocal trade agreements, revenue measures, tariffs and import quotas, and transportation of goods to which a duty is applied. The Senate Standing Committee on Finance has jurisdiction over the activities of a number of federal offices. The committee consists of several subcommittees, including the Subcommittee on Health Care, the Subcommittee on International Trade, the Subcommittee on Long-term Growth and Debt Reduction, the Subcommittee on Social Security and Family Policy, and the Subcommittee on Taxation and IRS Oversight.

Senate Standing Committee on Foreign Relations

The Senate Standing Committee on Foreign Relations was created in 1816 as one of ten original Senate committees. The committee has jurisdiction over issues pertaining to acquiring property for US embassies, US boundaries, diplomatic service, foreign economic, military, technical, and humanitarian assistance, foreign loans, the Red Cross when it is operating internationally, international matters related to nuclear energy, international conferences and congresses, international law, International Monetary Fund and other international monetary organizations, international intervention and war, efforts to foster US commercial interests internationally, national security, ocean and international environmental and scientific matters, protection of US citizens abroad, international relations, treaties, the United Nations, and the World Bank and other international development assistance organizations. Subcommittees include the Subcommittee on International Economic Policy, Export, and Trade Promotion; the Subcommittee on Near Eastern and South Asian Affairs; the Subcommittee on European Affairs; the Subcommittee on East Asian and Pacific Affairs; the Subcommittee on African Affairs; the Subcommittee on Western Hemisphere, Peace Corps, and Narcotics Affairs; and the Subcommittee on International Operations and Terrorism.

Senate Standing Committee on Health, Education, Labor, and Pensions

The Senate Standing Committee on Health, Education, Labor, and Pensions has jurisdiction over issues pertaining to education, labor, health, public welfare, aging, agricultural colleges, the arts and humanities, biomedical research and development, child labor, convict labor, the Red Cross when it is operating within the US, equal employment opportunity, Gallaudet College, Howard University, Saint Elizabeth's Hospital, people with disabilities, labor standards, labor statistics, settling labor disputes, occupational safety and health, private pension plans, public health, railway labor and retirement, foreign laborers, student loans, wages, and hours of labor. Subcommittees of the Senate Standing Committee on Health, Education, Labor, and Pensions include the Subcommittee on Retirement Security and Aging, the Subcommittee on Education and Early Childhood Development, the Subcommittee on Employment and Workplace Safety, and the Subcommittee on Bioterrorism and Public Health Preparedness.

Senate Standing Committee on Homeland Security and Governmental Affairs

The Senate Standing Committee on Homeland Security and Governmental Affairs has jurisdiction over issues pertaining to the Department of Homeland Security, the national archives, budget and accounting issues, the census and collecting statistics, Congressional organization, the Federal Civil Service, government information, intergovernmental relations, the District of Columbia, nuclear export policy, organization of the executive branch of the government, the postal service, and the status of officers and employees of the government. The subcommittees of the Senate Standing Committee on Homeland Security and Governmental Affairs include the Subcommittee on Federal Financial Management, Government Information, and International Security; the Permanent Subcommittee on Investigations; and the Subcommittee on Oversight of Government Management, the Federal Workforce, and the District of Columbia.

Senate Standing Committee on Judiciary

The Senate Standing Committee on Judiciary was created in 1816 as one of ten original Senate committees. The Senate Standing Committee on Judiciary has broad jurisdiction in the Senate over many matters, including jurisdiction over the **courts**. The committee also has jurisdiction over antitrust policy and competition policy, the rights of consumers, the Constitution, civil rights, and property rights. In addition, the Senate Standing Committee on Judiciary has jurisdiction over matters pertaining to corrections and rehabilitation and matters involving criminal activities and drugs, immigration, border security, citizenship, intellectual property rights, terrorism, technology, and homeland security.

Senate Standing Committee on Rules and Administration

The Senate Standing Committee on Rules and Administration has jurisdiction over issues pertaining to the administration of the Senate Office Buildings, the Senate branch of the Capitol Building, the rules and procedures that are used to organize Congress, Senate rules and regulations, corrupt activities, qualifications for Senators, federal elections, the government printing office and the printing of the Congressional record, Congressional meetings, attendance at Congressional meetings, use of funds from the Senate contingent fund, succession to the office of President, the procurement of books and manuscripts and the establishment of monuments and memorials, the Senate Library and artifacts in the Senate Office Buildings and in the Senate branch of the Capitol, services provided to the Senate, the US Capitol and congressional office buildings, the Library of Congress, the Smithsonian, and the Botanic Gardens.

Senate Standing Committee on Small Business and Entrepreneurship

The Senate Standing Committee on Small Business and Entrepreneurship was created in 1981 as the successor to the Select Committee on Small Business. The Senate Standing Committee on Small Business and Entrepreneurship has jurisdiction over the **Small Business Administration**. The Senate Standing Committee on Small Business and Entrepreneurship also has jurisdiction over legislation that is pertaining to other issues extending beyond those addressed by the Small Business Administration but that are requested to be investigated by the Senate Standing Committee on Small Business and Entrepreneurship. The Senate Standing Committee on Small Business and Entrepreneurship Study is also responsible for investigating topics of concern to small businesses in the United States.

Senate Standing Committee on Veterans Affairs

The Senate Standing Committee on Veterans Affairs was established in 1970. The committee has jurisdiction over the compensation of veterans, the life insurance provided to veterans of the armed forces by the United States government, national cemeteries, the pensions of all wars of the United States, the acclimation of individuals who have served in the armed forces back into civilian life, civil relief for soldiers and sailors, the administration of veterans hospitals, medical care for veterans, in a broad sense all efforts made on behalf of veterans, and vocational training and educational services provided to veterans.

Senate Committee on Indian Affairs

The Senate Committee on Indian Affairs was permanently established in 1984 after years as a temporary committee. The Senate Committee on Indian Affairs has jurisdiction over investigating the matters that pertain to the **Native American**, **Native Hawaiian**, and **Alaska Native** populations in the United States. The committee also has jurisdiction to propose legislation that is aimed at relieving matters of difficulty for these populations. Some of the matters that have been addressed by the committee are education for Native American populations, economic development, land management, trust responsibilities, health care, and cases made by Native Americans against the US government.

Senate Select Committee on Ethics

The Senate Select Committee on Ethics has jurisdiction over issues pertaining to the **Senate Code of Conduct**. The committee implements the ethics program for the Senate, as each branch of the federal government has the responsibility of implementing its own ethics program. Each house of the legislative branch has its own ethics committee to implement its ethics program; the counterpart to the Senate Select Committee on Ethics is the House Committee on Standards of Official Conduct. Specifically, the Senate Select Committee on Ethics addresses issues involving the ethics and conduct of individuals associated with the Senate that are related to financial disclosure, gifts, travel reimbursements, honoraria bans, constraints on outside employment, conflicting interests, constraints on employment activities after serving the Senate, campaign activities, money for Senate-related business, mailings, employment practices, interventions with other government agencies, and annual budget limits.

Senate Select Committee on Intelligence

The Senate Select Committee on Intelligence was established to investigate and to provide oversight of **US government intelligence activities and programs**. The committee is responsible for conducting investigations and providing them to the Senate, which in turn can use the materials that were gathered in the investigations to generate legislative proposals. The committee is also responsible for providing reports to the Senate on US government intelligence activities and programs. The committee is charged with ensuring that US government agencies that are involved with intelligence activities provide information on intelligence that is required for the executive branch and the legislative branch to develop well-informed policies and to make good decisions regarding national security. The committee also has the responsibility of providing oversight of US government intelligence activities to make sure that they are consistent with and comply with the US Constitution and laws.

Senate Special Committee on Aging

The Senate Special Committee on Aging was originally a temporary committee that was created in 1961, but it became a permanent committee in 1977. Because of its status as a special committee, it does not possess legislative authority. However, it can investigate matters of pertinence, and it does have the ability to oversee relevant programs. The Senate Special Committee on Aging addresses issues that are pertinent to older Americans. The committee provides the results of its investigations to the Senate and also makes legislative recommendations to the Senate. The committee also publishes documents that address public policies that are relevant to older Americans. The committee studies issues related to Medicare, pensions, and employment for older Americans. It also works to stop fraudulent activities that are aimed at the elderly.

Election Process, Length of Term, Qualifications, and Powers of the Senate

Senators are elected for terms of **six years**. The Senate is composed of **two** Senators from each state. Every two years, one-third of the Senate is up for re-election. Senators were originally chosen by their state legislatures, but with the passing of the **17th Amendment** in 1913, Senators are now elected directly by voters within their state. A Senator must be at least 30 years old, a citizen of the United States for at least nine years, and a resident of the state to which they are elected. The Senate has the power to try all impeachments.

Oversight Powers of Congress

Congress is afforded certain **oversight powers** that enable it to exert influence over the Executive branch of the US government. Congressional oversight is significant for a number of reasons; it stops waste and fraud, upholds civil liberties and rights, makes sure that the executive branch is in compliance with the law, serves as a means of gathering data and information that is necessary to make laws and to inform the public, and provides a means for evaluating the performance of the executive branch of government. Congressional oversight is applicable to the Cabinet, to all executive agencies, to regulatory commissions, and to the President.

Types of Congressional Oversight

There are a number of ways that Congress can exercise **oversight** of the executive branch of government in order to ensure a system of **checks and balances** and to exert influence over **public policy**. Some of the mechanisms available to Congress include the use of committee hearings, discussions and meetings with the President and other executive officials, reports from the President, the power of the Senate to advise and approve nominations made and treaties drafted by the President and to hold trials for impeached officials, the power of the House to impeach, the ability of Congress to address the order of succession of the Presidency, membership in government commissions, and studies by Congressional committees and Congressional support agencies.

Authorization and Appropriations

Authorization laws create, perpetuate, or alter federal programs, and they are required by House and Senate rules or laws before Congress can appropriate funds in the federal budget for the programs. **Direct spending**, also known as mandatory spending, involves expenditures for programs that are authorized by legislation that concurrently includes budget authority for the expenditures. **Discretionary spending** involves expenditures that are set annually by Congress. Discretionary spending is optional, as opposed to mandatory funding. An authorization can be permanent until Congress changes it, or an authorization can be applicable only in particular fiscal years. When an authorization expires, Congress can reauthorize the authorization through the legislative process. If an **appropriation** is made after the associated authorization expires, it is referred to as an unauthorized appropriation.

Joint Committee on Printing

The Joint Committee on Printing has the responsibility of overseeing the activities of the **United States Government Printing Office**. In addition, the **Joint Committee on Printing** has jurisdiction and oversight over all of the printing processes and procedures that are used within the federal government. The Joint Committee on Printing must make sure that all federal government organizations and individuals who represent the federal government are acting in accordance with the laws that are relevant to printing, and it must also make sure that all government organizations and individuals representing the government comply with Government Printing and Binding Regulations.

Joint Committee on Taxation

The Joint Committee is made up of ten members. Five members are from the Senate Committee on Finance, three of which represent the majority and two which represent the minority; the remaining five members are from the House Committee on Ways and Means, and again three of these represent the majority and two represent the minority. The committee has a key role in the **legislative process** as it pertains to **taxes**. The committee investigates internal revenue taxes, investigates efforts that could be made to simplify taxes, provides reports summarizing its investigations to the House Committee on Ways and Means and the Senate Committee on Finance and makes legislative recommendations, and reviews tax refunds that exceed two million dollars. The committee is required to provide a yearly report to Congress that lists refunds that exceed two million dollars, including the names of the individuals and businesses that are associated with these refunds and the exact amounts that are refunded.

Joint Committee on the Library

The Joint Committee on the Library is responsible for overseeing issues pertaining to the **Library of Congress**. The committee consists of five members, each from both the Senate and the House of Representatives, for a total of ten members. Specifically, membership consists of the chair and four members of the Senate Committee on Rules and Administration, as well as the chair and four members of the Committee on House Administration. The seat of the chair is alternately held by a member of the House of Representatives or the Senate each time that Congress convenes. There are no subcommittees for the Joint Committee on the Library. The committee was created in 1802 for the purpose of assisting with the expansion of a congressional library. Today, in addition to overseeing the Library of Congress, the committee also has jurisdiction over the art collection of Congress and the Botanic Garden. The committee can accept works of art on behalf of Congress and assign a spot in the US Capitol to display the art.

Joint Economic Committee

The Joint Economic Committee was established in 1946 when Congress passed the Employment Act of 1946. It was one of two advisory committees established under the **Employment Act of 1946**. The other committee established under this act was the President's Council of Economic Advisers. The purpose of both of these committees is to study and investigate economic conditions and to make recommendations regarding possible efforts to better **economic policy**. The Joint Economic Committee is chaired by either a member of the Senate or a member of the House of Representatives; each time Congress convenes, the chair alternates between the two chambers of Congress.

A Bill

A bill is a piece of legislation that is formally introduced in Congress. A bill can originate in either the House of Representatives or in the Senate. When a bill originates in the House of Representatives, it is designated as **H.R**. When a bill originates in the Senate it is designated by **S**. Bills are numbered in consecutive order. Bills can be categorized into either public bills or private bills. **Public bills** address general issues. If a public bill is both approved by Congress and signed by the President, it is passed and becomes a Public Law, or a Public Act. In contrast, **private bills** address individual circumstances. For example, private bills might be introduced to address a case against the Federal Government, immigration and naturalization cases, or land titles. If a private bill is both approved by Congress and signed by the President, it is passed and becomes a private law.

How Laws are Passed

Bills for raising **revenue**, such as those for taxes, originate in the House of Representatives. All bills must pass both the Senate and the House of Representatives in the exact same form. A bill that passes in both houses is sent to the President, who can either sign the bill or veto it. If the President **signs** the bill, it becomes law. If the President **vetoes** the bill, it is sent back to Congress, and if both the House and the Senate pass it by a two-thirds majority, the bill becomes law, thereby overriding the President's veto. If the President neither vetoes a bill nor signs it within ten days after receiving it from Congress, it becomes a law without his signature. However, if Congress sends a bill to the President and then adjourns, it does not become law if the President does not sign the bill within ten days; this is known as a **pocket veto**.

US Government and Citizenship

Political Science and Its Ties to Other Major Disciplines

Political science focuses on studying different governments and how they compare to each other, general political theory, ways political theory is put into action, how nations and governments interact with each other, and a general study of governmental structure and function. Other elements of **political science** include the study of elections, governmental administration at various levels, development and action of political parties, and how values such as freedom, power, justice, and equality are expressed in different political cultures. Political science also encompasses elements of other disciplines, including:

- **History**—how historical events have shaped political thought and process
- **Sociology**—the effects of various stages of social development on the growth and development of government and politics
- **Anthropology**—the effects of governmental process on the culture of an individual group and its relationships with other groups
- **Economics**—how government policies regulate the distribution of products and how they can control and/or influence the economy in general

General Political Theory

Based on general political theory, the four major purposes of any given government are:

- **Ensuring national security**—the government protects against international, domestic, and terrorist attacks and also ensures ongoing security through negotiating and establishing relationships with other governments.
- **Providing public services**—the government should "promote the general welfare," as stated in the Preamble to the US Constitution, by providing whatever is needed to its citizens.
- **Ensuring social order**—the government supplies means of settling conflicts among citizens as well as making laws to govern the nation, state, or city.
- **Making decisions regarding the economy**—laws help form the economic policy of the country, regarding both domestic and international trade and related issues. The government also has the ability to distribute goods and wealth to some extent among its citizens.

Main Theories Regarding the Origin of the State

There are four main theories regarding the origin of the state:

- **Evolutionary**—the state evolved from the family, with the head of state the equivalent of the family's patriarch or matriarch.
- **Force**—one person or group of people brought everyone in an area under their control, forming the first government.
- **Divine Right**—certain people were chosen by the prevailing deity to be the rulers of the nation, which is itself created by the deity or deities.
- **Social Contract**—there is no natural order. The people allow themselves to be governed to maintain social order, while the state, in turn, promises to protect the people they govern. If the government fails to protect its people, the people have the right to seek new leaders.

Public Policy

Public policy is the study of how the various levels of government formulate and implement policies. **Public policy** also refers to the set of policies that a government adopts and implements, including laws, plans, actions, and behaviors, for the purpose of governing society. Public policy is developed and adapted through the process of **policy analysis**. Public policy analysis is the systematic evaluation of alternative means of reaching social goals. Public policy is divided into various policy areas, including domestic policy, foreign policy, healthcare policy, education policy, criminal policy, national defense policy, and energy policy.

Influences of Philosophers on Political Study

Ancient Greek philosophers **Aristotle** and **Plato** believed political science would lead to order in political matters and that this scientifically organized order would create stable, just societies.

- **Thomas Aquinas** adapted the ideas of Aristotle to a Christian perspective. His ideas stated that individuals should have certain rights but also certain duties, and that these rights and duties should determine the type and extent of government rule. In stating that laws should limit the role of government, he laid the groundwork for ideas that would eventually become modern constitutionalism.
- **Niccolò Machiavelli**, author of *The Prince*, was a proponent of politics based on power. He is often considered the founder of modern political science.
- **Thomas Hobbes**, author of *Leviathan* (1651), believed that individuals' lives were focused solely on a quest for power and that the state must work to control this urge. Hobbes felt that people were completely unable to live harmoniously without the intervention of a powerful, undivided government.

Contributions of John Locke, Montesquieu, and Rousseau to Political Science

John Locke published *Two Treatises of Government* in 1689. This work argued against the ideas of Thomas Hobbes. He put forth the theory of *tabula rasa*—that people are born with minds like blank slates. Individual minds are molded by experience, not innate knowledge or intuition. He also believed that all men should be independent and equal. Many of Locke's ideas found their way into the Constitution of the United States.

The two French philosophers, **Montesquieu** and **Rousseau**, heavily influenced the French Revolution (1789-1799). They believed government policies and ideas should change to alleviate existing problems, an idea referred to as "liberalism." Rousseau, in particular, directly influenced the Revolution with writings such as *The Social Contract* (1762) and *Declaration of the Rights of Man and of the Citizen* (1789). Other ideas Rousseau and Montesquieu espoused included:

- Individual freedom and community welfare are of equal importance
- Man's innate goodness leads to natural harmony
- Reason develops with the rise of civilized society
- Individual citizens carry certain obligations to the existing government

Political Ideologies of Famous Philosophers

David Hume and **Jeremy Bentham** believed politics should have as its main goal maintaining "the greatest happiness for the greatest number." Hume also believed in empiricism, or that ideas should not be believed until the proof has been observed. He was a natural skeptic and always sought out the truth of matters rather than believing what he was told.

John Stuart Mill, a British philosopher and economist, made significant contributions to the fields of social and economic theory. A majorly influential thinker in the realm of classical liberalism, Mill believed in progressive policies such as women's suffrage, emancipation, and the development of labor unions and farming cooperatives. His ideas on free speech and the harm principle were the basis for the "clear and present danger" test outlined by Oliver Wendell Holmes Jr. when determining if speech is protected by the First Amendment of the US Constitution.

Johann Fichte and **Georg Hegel**, German philosophers in the late 18th and early 19th centuries, supported a form of liberalism grounded largely in socialism and a sense of nationalism.

Main Political Orientations

The four main political orientations are:

- **Liberal**—liberals believe that government should work to increase equality, even at the expense of some freedoms. Government should assist those in need, focusing on enforced social justice and free basic services for everyone.
- **Conservative**—a conservative believes that government should be limited in most cases. The government should allow its citizens to help one another and solve their own problems rather than enforcing solutions. Business should not be overregulated, allowing a free market.
- **Moderate**—this ideology incorporates some liberal and some conservative values, generally falling somewhere between in overall belief.
- **Libertarian**—libertarians believe that the government's role should be limited to protecting the life and liberty of citizens. Government should not be involved in any citizen's life unless that citizen is encroaching upon the rights of another.

Major Principles of Government as Outlined in the United States Constitution

The six major principles of government as outlined in the United States Constitution are:

- **Federalism**—the power of the government does not belong entirely to the national government but is divided between federal and state governments.
- **Popular sovereignty**—the government is determined by the people and gains its authority and power from the people.
- **Separation of powers**—the government is divided into three branches (executive, legislative, and judicial) with each having its own set of powers.
- **Judicial review**—courts at all levels of government can declare laws invalid if they contradict the constitutions of individual states, or the US Constitution, with the Supreme Court serving as the final judicial authority on decisions of this kind.
- **Checks and balances**—no single branch can act without input from another, and each branch has the power to "check" any other, as well as balance other branches' powers.
- **Limited government**—governmental powers are limited, and certain individual rights are defined as inviolable by the government.

Types of Powers Delegated to the National Government by the US Constitution

The structure of the US government divides power between national and state governments. Powers delegated to the federal government by the Constitution are:

- **Expressed powers**—powers directly defined in the Constitution, including power to declare war, regulate commerce, make money, and collect taxes
- **Implied powers**—powers the national government must have in order to carry out the expressed powers
- **Inherent powers**—powers inherent to any government, not expressly defined in the Constitution

Some of these powers, such as collection and levying of taxes, are also granted to the individual state governments.

Primary Positions of Federalism and Development through the Years in the US

The way federalism should be practiced has been the subject of debate since the writing of the Constitution. There were—and still are—two main factions regarding this issue:

- **States' rights**—those favoring the states' rights position feel that the state governments should take the lead in performing local actions to manage various problems.
- **Nationalist**—those favoring a nationalist position feel the national government should take the lead to deal with those same matters.

The flexibility of the Constitution has allowed the US government to shift and adapt as the needs of the country have changed. Power has often shifted from the state governments to the national government and back again, and both levels of government have developed various ways to influence each other.

Effects of Federalism on Policy-Making and the Balance of Politics in the US

Federalism has three major effects on **public policy** in the US:

- Determining whether the local, state, or national government originates policy
- Affecting how policies are made
- Ensuring policy-making functions under a set of limitations

Federalism also influences the **political balance of power** in the US by:

- Making it difficult, if not impossible, for a single political party to seize total power
- Ensuring that individuals can participate in the political system at various levels
- Making it possible for individuals working within the system to be able to affect policy at some level, whether local or more widespread

Three Branches of the US Federal Government

The following are the three branches of the US Federal government and the individuals that belong to each branch:

- **Legislative Branch**—this consists of the two houses of Congress: the House of Representatives and the Senate. All members of the Legislative Branch are elected officials.
- **Executive Branch**—this branch is made up of the president, vice president, presidential advisors, and other various cabinet members. Advisors and cabinet members are appointed by the president, but they must be approved by Congress.
- **Judicial Branch**—the federal court system, headed by the Supreme Court.

Review Video: What Does the Executive Branch Do?
Visit mometrix.com/academy and enter code: 210629

Review Video: What Does the Judicial Branch Do?
Visit mometrix.com/academy and enter code: 278093

Review Video: What Does the Legislative Branch Do?
Visit mometrix.com/academy and enter code: 405303

Major Responsibilities of the Three Branches of the Federal Government

The three branches of the federal government each have specific roles and responsibilities:

- The **Legislative Branch** is largely concerned with lawmaking. All laws must be approved by Congress before they go into effect. They are also responsible for regulating money and trade, approving presidential appointments, and establishing organizations like the postal service and federal courts. Congress can also propose amendments to the Constitution, and can impeach, or bring charges against, the president. Only Congress can declare war.
- The **Executive Branch** carries out laws, treaties, and war declarations enacted by Congress. The president can also veto bills approved by Congress, and serves as commander in chief of the US military. The president appoints cabinet members, ambassadors to foreign countries, and federal judges.

- The **Judicial Branch** makes decisions on challenges as to whether laws passed by Congress meet the requirements of the US Constitution. The Supreme Court may also choose to review decisions made by lower courts to determine their constitutionality.

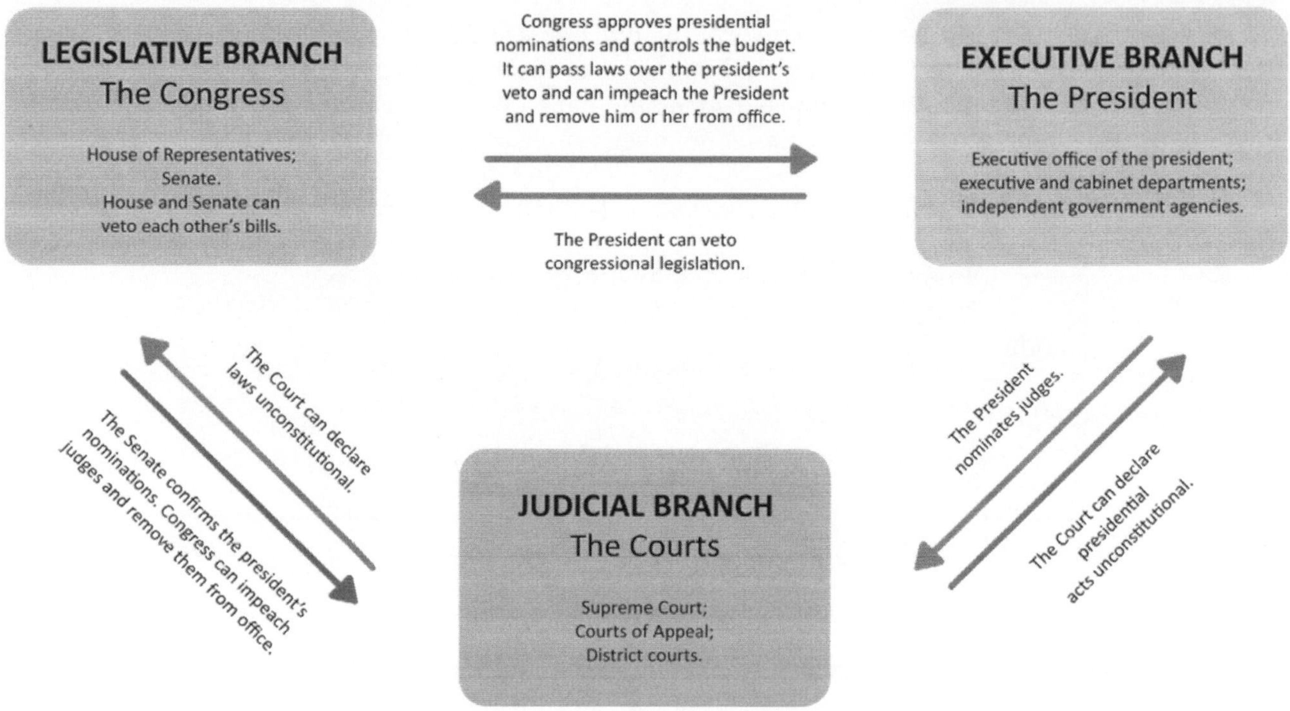

US CITIZENSHIP

QUALIFICATIONS OF A US CITIZEN/HOW CITIZENSHIP MAY BE LOST

Anyone born in the US, born abroad to a US citizen, or who has gone through a process of naturalization is considered a **citizen** of the United States. It is possible to lose US citizenship as a result of conviction of certain crimes such as treason. Citizenship may also be lost if a citizen pledges an oath to another country or serves in the military of a country engaged in hostilities with the US. A US citizen can also choose to hold dual citizenship, work as an expatriate in another country without losing US citizenship, or even to renounce citizenship if he or she so chooses.

RIGHTS, DUTIES, AND RESPONSIBILITIES GRANTED TO OR EXPECTED FROM CITIZENS

Citizens are granted certain rights under the US government. The most important of these are defined in the **Bill of Rights**, and include freedom of speech, religion, assembly, and a variety of other rights the government is not allowed to remove. A US citizen also has a number of **duties**:

- Paying taxes
- Loyalty to the government (though the US does not prosecute those who criticize or seek to change the government)
- Support and defense of the Constitution
- Serving in the Armed Forces when required by law
- Obeying laws as set forth by the various levels of government.

Responsibilities of a US citizen include:

- Voting in elections
- Respecting one another's rights and not infringing on them

- Staying informed about various political and national issues
- Respecting one another's beliefs

Bill of Rights

Importance of the Bill of Rights

The first ten amendments of the US Constitution are known as the **Bill of Rights**. These amendments prevent the government from infringing upon certain freedoms that the Founding Fathers felt were natural rights that already belonged to all people. These rights included freedom of speech, freedom of religion, freedom of assembly, and the right to bear arms. Many of the rights were formulated in direct response to the way the colonists felt they had been mistreated by the British government.

Rights Granted in the Bill of Rights

The first ten amendments were passed by Congress in 1789. Three-fourths of the existing thirteen states had ratified them by December of 1791, making them official additions to the Constitution. The rights granted in the Bill of Rights are:

- **First Amendment**—freedom of religion, speech, freedom of the press, and the right to assemble and to petition the government
- **Second Amendment**—the right to bear arms
- **Third Amendment**—Congress cannot force individuals to house troops
- **Fourth Amendment**—protection from unreasonable search and seizure
- **Fifth Amendment**—no individual is required to testify against himself, and no individual may be tried twice for the same crime
- **Sixth Amendment**—the right to criminal trial by jury and the right to legal counsel
- **Seventh Amendment**—the right to civil trial by jury
- **Eighth Amendment**—protection from excessive bail or cruel and unusual punishment
- **Ninth Amendment**—prevents rights not explicitly named in the Constitution from being taken away because they are not named
- **Tenth Amendment**—any rights not directly delegated to the national government, or not directly prohibited by the government from the states, belong to the states or to the people

Review Video: Bill of Rights
Visit mometrix.com/academy and enter code: 585149

Situations Where the Government Restricts the First Amendment Freedoms

In some cases, the government restricts certain elements of First Amendment rights. Some examples include:

- **Freedom of religion**—when a religion espouses illegal activities, the government often restricts these forms of religious expression. Examples include polygamy, animal sacrifice, and use of illicit drugs or illegal substances.
- **Freedom of speech**—this can be restricted if exercise of free speech endangers other people.
- **Freedom of the press**—laws prevent the press from publishing falsehoods.

In **emergency situations** such as wartime, stricter restrictions are sometimes placed on these rights, especially rights to free speech and assembly, and freedom of the press, in order to protect national security.

Constitution's Address of the Rights of Those Accused of Crimes

The US Constitution makes allowances for the **rights of criminals**, or anyone who has transgressed established laws. There must be laws to protect citizens from criminals, but those accused of crimes must also be protected and their basic rights as individuals preserved. In addition, the Constitution protects individuals from the power of authorities to prevent police forces and other enforcement organizations from becoming oppressive. The fourth, fifth, sixth, and eighth amendments specifically address these rights.

Supreme Court's Provision of Equal Protection for All Individuals

When the Founding Fathers wrote in the Declaration of Independence that "all men are created equal," they actually were referring to men, and, in fact, defined citizens as white men who owned land. However, as the country has developed and changed, the definition has expanded to more wholly include all people.

"**Equality**" does not mean all people are inherently the same, but it does mean they all should be granted the same rights and should be treated the same by the government. Amendments to the Constitution have granted citizenship and voting rights to all Americans regardless of race or gender. The Supreme Court evaluates various laws and court decisions to determine if they properly represent the idea of **equal protection**. One sample case was Brown v. Board of Education in 1954, which declared separate-but-equal treatment to be unconstitutional.

Protests

A protest is an expression of opposition to, and sometimes of support of, events or circumstances. **Protests** represent a means for individuals to publicly make their views heard in an effort to influence public opinion or government policy, or as a means to enact **change**. Protests generally result when self-expression of opposing views is restricted by government policy, political or economic circumstances, religion, social structures, or the media, and people react by declaring their views through cultural mechanisms or on the streets. There are numerous forms of protest, including boycotts, civil disobedience, demonstrations, non-violent protests, picketing, protest marches, protest songs, riots, sit-ins, teach-ins, strikes, and others.

Civil Liberty Challenges Addressed in Current Political Discussions

The **civil rights movements** of the 1960s and the ongoing struggle for the rights of women and other minorities have sparked **challenges to existing law**. In addition, debate has raged over how much information the government should be required to divulge to the public. Major issues in the 21st century political climate include:

- Continued debate over women's rights, especially regarding equal pay for equal work
- Debate over affirmative action to encourage hiring of minorities
- Debate over civil rights of homosexuals, including marriage and military service
- Decisions as to whether minorities should be compensated for past discriminatory practices
- Balance between the public's right to know and the government's need to maintain national security
- Balance between the public's right to privacy and national security

Civil Liberties vs. Civil Rights

While the terms *civil liberties* and *civil rights* are often used interchangeably, in actuality, their definitions are slightly different. The two concepts work together, however, to define the basics of a free state:

- **"Civil liberties"** define the constitutional freedoms guaranteed to citizens. Examples include freedoms such as free speech, privacy, or free thought.
- **"Civil rights"** are guarantees of or protections of civil liberties. One comparison can be found in the case of freedom of religion. The civil liberty is that one has the freedom to practice the religion of his or her choice, whereas the civil right would protect that individual from being denied a job on the basis of their religion.

Suffrage, Franchise, and the Change of Voting Rights Over American History

Suffrage and franchise both refer to the right to **vote**. As the US developed as a nation, there was much debate over which individuals should hold this right. In the early years, only white male landowners were granted suffrage. By the 19th century, most states had franchised, or granted the right to vote, to all adult white males. The **Fifteenth Amendment** of 1870 granted suffrage to formerly enslaved men. The **Nineteenth Amendment** gave women the right to vote in 1920, and in 1971 the **Twenty-sixth Amendment** expanded voting rights to include any US citizen over the age of eighteen. However, those who have not been granted full citizenship and citizens who have committed certain crimes do not have voting rights.

Ways in Which the Voting Process Has Changed Over the Years

The first elections in the US were held by **public ballot**. However, election abuses soon became common, since public ballot made it easy to intimidate, threaten, or otherwise influence the votes of individuals or groups of individuals. New practices were put into play, including **registering voters** before elections took place and using a **secret or Australian ballot**. In 1892, the introduction of the **voting machine** further privatized the voting process, since it allowed complete privacy for voting. Today, debate continues about the accuracy of various voting methods, including high-tech voting machines and even low-tech punch cards.

Effect of Political Parties on the Functioning of an Individual Government

Different types and numbers of political parties can have a significant effect on how a government is run. If there is a **single party**, or a one-party system, the government is defined by that one party, and all policy is based on that party's beliefs. In a **two-party system**, two parties with different viewpoints compete for power and influence. The US is basically a two-party system, with checks and balances to make it difficult for one party to gain complete power over the other. There are also **multiparty systems**, with three or more parties. In multiparty systems, various parties will often come to agreements in order to form a majority and shift the balance of power.

Development of Political Parties in the US.

George Washington was adamantly against the establishment of **political parties**, based on the abuses perpetrated by such parties in Britain. However, political parties developed in US politics almost from the beginning. Major parties throughout US history have included:

- **Federalists and Democratic-Republicans**—these parties formed in the late 1700s and disagreed on the balance of power between national and state government.
- **Democrats and Whigs**—these developed in the 1830s, and many political topics of the time centered on national economic issues.
- **Democrats and Republicans**—the Republican Party developed before the Civil War, after the collapse of the Whig party, and the two parties debated issues centering on slavery and economic issues, such as taxation.

While third parties sometimes enter the picture in US politics, the government is basically a two-party system, dominated by the Democrats and Republicans.

Functions of Political Parties

Political parties form organizations at all levels of government. Activities of individual parties include:

- Recruiting and backing candidates for offices
- Discussing various issues with the public, increasing public awareness
- Working toward compromise on difficult issues
- Staffing government offices and providing administrative support

At the administrative level, parties work to ensure that viable candidates are available for elections and that offices and staff are in place to support candidates as they run for office and afterward, when they are elected.

Processes of Selecting Political Candidates

Historically, in the quest for political office, a potential candidate has followed one of the following four processes:

- **Nominating convention**—an official meeting of the members of a party for the express purpose of nominating candidates for upcoming elections. The Democratic National Convention and the Republican National Convention, convened to announce candidates for the presidency, are examples of this kind of gathering.
- **Caucus**—a meeting, usually attended by a party's leaders. Some states still use caucuses, but not all.
- **Primary election**—the most common method of choosing candidates today, the primary is a publicly held election to choose candidates.
- **Petition**—signatures gathered to place a candidate on the ballot. Petitions can also be used to place legislation on a ballot.

Ways the Average Citizen Participates in the Political Process

In addition to voting for elected officials, American citizens are able to participate in the political process through several other avenues. These include:

- Participating in local government
- Participating in caucuses for large elections

- Volunteering to help political parties
- Running for election to local, state, or national offices

Individuals can also donate money to political causes or support political groups that focus on specific causes such as abortion, wildlife conservation, or women's rights. These groups often make use of **representatives** who lobby legislators to act in support of their efforts.

Ways in Which Political Campaign Gains Funding

Political campaigns are very expensive. In addition to the basic necessities of a campaign office, including office supplies, office space, etc., a large quantity of the money that funds a political campaign goes toward **advertising**. Money to fund a political campaign can come from several sources, including:

- The candidate's personal funds
- Donations by individuals
- Special interest groups

The most significant source of campaign funding is **special interest groups**. Groups in favor of certain policies will donate money to candidates they believe will support those policies. Special interest groups also do their own advertising in support of candidates they endorse.

Presidential Elections

The President of the United States is elected **indirectly** by members of an **electoral college**. Members of the electoral college nearly always vote along the lines of the popular vote of their respective states. The winner of a presidential election is the candidate with at least 270 **Electoral College votes**. It is possible for a candidate to win the electoral vote and lose the popular vote. Incumbent Presidents and challengers typically prefer a balanced ticket, where the President and Vice President are elected together and generally balance one another with regard to geography, ideology, or experience working in government. The nominated Vice Presidential candidate is referred to as the President's **running mate**.

Importance of Free Press and the Media

The right to free speech guaranteed in the first amendment to the Constitution allows the media to report on **government and political activities** without fear of retribution. Because the media has access to information about the government, the government's policies and actions, and debates and discussions that occur in Congress, it can keep the public informed about the inner workings of the government. The media can also draw attention to injustices, imbalances of power, and other transgressions the government or government officials might commit. However, media outlets may, like special interest groups, align themselves with certain political viewpoints and skew their reports to fit that viewpoint. The rise of the **internet** has made media reporting even more complex, as news can be found from an infinite variety of sources, both reliable and unreliable.

Forms of Government

Anarchism, Communism, and Dictatorship

Anarchists believe that all government should be eliminated and that individuals should rule themselves. Historically, anarchists have used violence and assassination to further their beliefs.

Communism is based on class conflict, revolution, and a one-party state. Ideally, a communist government would involve a single government for the entire world. Communist government controls the production and flow of goods and services rather than leaving this to companies or individuals.

Dictatorship involves rule by a single individual. If rule is enforced by a small group, this is referred to as an oligarchy. Dictators tend to rule with a violent hand, using a highly repressive police force to ensure control over the populace.

Fascism and Monarchy

Fascism centers on a single leader and is, ideologically, an oppositional belief to communism. **Fascism** includes a single-party state and centralized control. The power of the fascist leader lies in the "cult of personality," and the fascist state often focuses on expansion and conquering of other nations. **Monarchy** was the major form of government for Europe through most of its history.

A monarchy is led by a king or a queen. This position is hereditary, and the rulers are not elected. In modern times, constitutional monarchy has developed, where the king and queen still exist, but most of the governmental decisions are made by democratic institutions such as a parliament.

Parliamentary and Democratic Systems

In a parliamentary system, government involves a legislature and a variety of political parties. The head of government, usually a prime minister, is typically the head of the dominant party. A head of state can be elected, or this position can be taken by a monarch, as in Great Britain's constitutional monarchy system.

In a **democratic system** of government, the people elect their government representatives. The word *democracy* is a Greek term that means "rule of the people." There are two forms of democracy: direct and indirect. In a direct democracy, each issue or election is decided by a vote where each individual is counted separately. An indirect democracy employs a legislature that votes on issues that affect large numbers of people whom the legislative members represent. Democracy can exist as a parliamentary system or a presidential system. The US is a presidential, indirect democracy.

Presidential System and Socialism

A presidential system, like a parliamentary system, has a legislature and political parties, but there is no difference between the head of state and the head of government. Instead of separating these functions, an elected president performs both. Election of the president can be direct or indirect, and the president may not necessarily belong to the largest political party. In **socialism**, the state controls the production of goods, though it does not necessarily own all means of production. The state also provides a variety of social services to citizens and helps guide the economy. A democratic form of government often exists in socialist countries.

Review Video: Communism vs. Socialism
Visit mometrix.com/academy and enter code: 917677

Totalitarian and Authoritarian Systems

A totalitarian system believes everything should be under the control of the government—from resource production, to the press, to religion, and other social institutions. All aspects of life under a totalitarian system must conform to the ideals of the government. **Authoritarian** governments practice widespread state authority but do not necessarily dismantle all public institutions. If a church, for example, exists as an organization but poses no threat to the authority of the state, an authoritarian government might leave it as it is. While all totalitarian governments are by definition authoritarian, a government can be authoritarian without becoming totalitarian.

Review Video: Totalitarianism vs. Authoritarianism
Visit mometrix.com/academy and enter code: 104046

Parliamentary and Democratic Systems

In a parliamentary system, government involves a legislature and a variety of political parties. The head of government, usually a prime minister, is typically the head of the dominant party. A head of state can be elected, or this position can be taken by a monarch, as in Great Britain's constitutional monarchy system.

In a **democratic system** of government, the people elect their government representatives. The word *democracy* is a Greek term that means "rule of the people." There are two forms of democracy: direct and indirect. In a direct democracy, each issue or election is decided by a vote where each individual is counted separately. An indirect democracy employs a legislature that votes on issues that affect large numbers of people whom the legislative members represent. Democracy can exist as a parliamentary system or a presidential system. The US is a presidential, indirect democracy.

Realism, Liberalism, Institutionalism, and Constructivism

The theory of realism states that nations are by nature aggressive and work in their own self-interest. Relations between nations are determined by military and economic strength. The nation is seen as the highest authority. **Liberalism** believes states can cooperate and that they act based on capability rather than power. This term was originally coined to describe Woodrow Wilson's theories on international cooperation. In **institutionalism**, institutions provide structure and incentive for cooperation among nations. Institutions are defined as a set of rules used to make international decisions. These institutions also help distribute power and determine how nations will interact. **Constructivism**, like liberalism, is based on international cooperation but recognizes that perceptions countries have of each other can affect their relations.

Effects of Foreign Policy on a Country's Position in World Affairs

Foreign policy is a set of goals, policies, and strategies that determine how an individual nation will interact with other countries. These strategies shift, sometimes quickly and drastically, according to actions or changes occurring in the other countries. However, a nation's **foreign policy** is often based on a certain set of ideals and national needs. Examples of US foreign policy include isolationism versus internationalism. In the 1800s, the US leaned more toward isolationism, exhibiting a reluctance to become involved in foreign affairs. The World Wars led to a period of internationalism, as the US entered these wars in support of other countries and joined the United Nations. Today's foreign policy tends more toward **interdependence**, or **globalism**, recognizing the widespread effects of issues like economic health.

Major Figures Involved in Determining and Enacting US Foreign Policy

US foreign policy is largely determined by Congress and the president, influenced by the secretary of state, secretary of defense, and the national security adviser. Executive officials carry out policies. The main departments in charge of these day-to-day issues are the **US Department of State**, also referred to as the State Department. The Department of State carries out policy, negotiates treaties, maintains diplomatic relations, assists citizens traveling in foreign countries, and ensures that the president is properly informed of any international issues. The **Department of Defense**, the largest executive department in the US, supervises the armed forces and provides assistance to the president in his role as commander-in-chief.

Major Types of International Organizations

Two types of international organizations are:

- **Intergovernmental organizations (IGOs)**. These organizations are made up of members from various national governments. The UN is an example of an intergovernmental organization. Treaties among the member nations determine the functions and powers of these groups.
- **Nongovernmental organizations (NGOs)**. An NGO lies outside the scope of any government and is usually supported through private donations. An example of an NGO is the International Red Cross, which works with governments all over the world when their countries are in crisis but is formally affiliated with no particular country or government.

Role of Diplomats in International Relations

Diplomats are individuals who reside in foreign countries in order to maintain communications between that country and their home country. They help negotiate trade agreements and environmental policies, as well as conveying official information to foreign governments. They also help to resolve conflicts between the countries, often working to sort out issues without making the conflicts official in any way. **Diplomats**, or **ambassadors**, are appointed in the US by the president. Appointments must be approved by Congress.

Role of the United Nations in International Relations and Diplomacy

The United Nations (**UN**) helps form international policies by hosting representatives of various countries who then provide input into policy decisions. Countries that are members of the UN must agree to abide by all final UN resolutions, but this is not always the case in practice, as dissent is not uncommon. If countries do not follow UN resolutions, the UN can decide on sanctions against those countries, often economic sanctions, such as trade restriction. The UN can also send military forces to problem areas, with "peacekeeping" troops brought in from member nations. An example of this function is the Korean War, the first war in which an international organization played a major role.

Chapter Quiz

Ready to see how well you retained what you just read? Scan the QR code to go directly to the chapter quiz interface for this study guide. If you're using a computer, simply visit the online resources page at **mometrix.com/resources719/clepamergov** and click the Chapter Quizzes link.

Federal Courts, Civil Liberties, and Civil Rights

United States Federal Government Judicial Branch

Judicial Branch

The United States Judicial Branch was established with the creation of the US Supreme Court, which was stipulated by **Article III** of the US Constitution. The **Supreme Court** is the highest court in the United States, and it is granted the judicial powers of the United States government. In addition to the Supreme Court, the judicial branch also consists of lower **Federal courts** that were created by Congress using its Constitutional powers. The responsibility of the Courts is to settle disputes about the meaning of laws and how laws are applied, and, through **judicial review**, to decide whether or not laws violate the US Constitution. It is through judicial review that the judicial branch exercises the system of checks and balances with regard to the executive and legislative branches.

Review Video: Duties of the Judicial Branch
Visit mometrix.com/academy and enter code: 278093

Powers of the Supreme Court

The **Supreme Court** is tasked with settling disputes involving the interpretation of the **Constitution**. The process of determining whether a law or action is in violation of the Constitution is **judicial review**. The Supreme Court can overturn both state and federal laws if they are determined to violate the Constitution. The decisions of the Supreme Court can only be altered by means of another Supreme Court decision or through an amendment to the Constitution. The Supreme Court has full authority over federal courts and restricted authority over state courts. The Supreme Court has the final say over cases heard by federal courts and also stipulates the procedures that federal courts must abide by. Although federal courts are required to uphold the Supreme Court's interpretations of federal laws and the Constitution and the Supreme Court's interpretations of federal law and the Constitution also apply to state courts, the Supreme Court cannot interpret state laws or Constitutions and doesn't oversee state court procedures.

Supreme Court Justices

Nine Justices currently comprise the Supreme Court; eight of these are referred to as **Associate Justices** and one is referred to as the **Chief Justice**. The number of Supreme Court Justices is set by Congress. The Supreme Court Justices are appointed by the President of the United States and with consent from the Senate. After individuals have been approved by the Senate and have been sworn in to the Supreme Court, they may keep the position of Supreme Court Justice for the remainder of their lives. Justices may leave their positions if they choose to resign or retire, or if they die, or if they are impeached. Historically, there has never been a Justice who has been removed from the Supreme Court through impeachment. There are not any specific requirements to become a Supreme Court Justice.

Appealing Cases in Higher Courts

Prior to being heard before the Supreme Court, cases are typically first heard before **lower courts**, including both state and federal courts. If a lower court makes a decision that the losing party in the case believes is unjust, that party has the option of appealing the case and bringing it before a higher court. At the state level, courts where appeals are heard are referred to as **appellate courts**.

At the federal level, lower courts are referred to as **United States District Courts** and higher courts are referred to as **United States Courts of Appeals**.

Supreme Court and Original Jurisdiction

Although it is rare for cases to originate in the Supreme Court, it does have the power of **original jurisdiction** to hear cases involving ambassadors and other foreign officials. Similarly, cases involving two or more states originate in the Supreme Court. If a decision made by a higher court is in disagreement with a decision made by a lower court, the decision made by the lower court is **overturned**. If a decision made by a higher court is in agreement with a decision made by a lower court, the losing party can request that the case be heard before the **Supreme Court**. However, only cases addressing federal or Constitutional law are heard before the Supreme Court.

Bringing a Case before the Supreme Court

The total number of cases sent to the Supreme Court annually is around 7,500. However, the Supreme Court typically only hears between eighty and one hundred of these cases. When a case is submitted to the Supreme Court, the Supreme Court Justices convene to determine whether the case should be heard before the Court. The criteria used to make this determination specifically include deciding whether the case addresses **federal law** or **Constitutional law**. In addition, the Justices must take into consideration the possibility that any decision made in the Supreme Court could affect the outcome of many cases heard before lower courts and subsequently make efforts to exercise this power only in cases involving a constitutional issue.

Supreme Court Hearing

The Supreme Court is in **session** from the first Monday in October through late June of the following year. If the Justices are not hearing cases, they conduct legal research and write opinions. On Fridays, Justices deliberate cases that they have heard and vote. If the Supreme Court Justices decide to hear a case, legal representation for each side has a half-hour to present an oral argument. Justices may ask questions throughout oral arguments. A majority of the Justices are required to decide a case. If the Chief Justice sides with the majority, he or she writes the **majority opinion**, or the Chief Justice assigns the task to another Justice on the majority side. If the Chief Justice does not side with the majority, the Justice who has served the longest on the Supreme Court writes the opinion or assigns the task to one of the other Justices. Opinions form the foundation for arguments in similar future cases, serving as **precedent**. Justices who are in the minority may write **dissenting opinions**.

Supreme Court Officers

The Supreme Court is aided by Court Officers, who help to ensure that the functions of the court are carried out smoothly. The **Court Officers** include the Administrative Assistant to the Chief Justice, who is appointed by the Chief Justice. In addition, the Court Officers include the Clerk, the Reporter of Decisions, the Librarian, and the Marshal, all of whom are appointed by the Supreme Court. The Court Officers also include the Director of Budget and Personnel, the Court Counsel, the Curator, the Director of Data Systems, and the Public Information Officer. These Court Officers are appointed by the **Chief Justice** with the advice of the rest of the Supreme Court.

Jurisdiction of the Federal Courts

The Constitution stipulates that the federal courts have jurisdiction over cases involving a number of issues. **Federal judicial power** extends to cases involving the United States Constitution, federal laws, and treaties. Federal courts deal with cases involving ambassadors and other foreign officials, cases involving admiralty and maritime issues, cases in which the United States federal government is a party, cases involving disputes between two or more states, cases involving disputes between a state and citizens of another state, cases involving disputes between citizens of different states, cases involving citizens from one state who are claiming land in different states, and cases involving disputes between a state or its citizens and foreign states or foreign citizens. The Supreme Court has **original jurisdiction** in cases involving ambassadors and other foreign ministers and in any case in which a state is a party. In all other cases, the Supreme Court has **appellate jurisdiction**.

Powers Denied and Restrictions on the Federal Government

There are a number of powers that the federal government is not granted. The federal government does not have the power to suspend the **Writ of Habeas Corpus**. The federal government does not have the power to pass a **Bill of Attainder** or an **ex post facto law**. The federal government is restricted from displaying preferential treatment for one state over others. The federal government does not have the power to spend money from the US Treasury before first receiving the approval of Congress. The federal government does not have the power to confer a title of nobility to any individual. An individual who holds a federal government office is restricted from accepting gifts from foreign countries; this restriction exists to prevent offers that might constitute bribes.

How Laws are Made

Part I

Laws can originate in either the House of Representatives or the Senate. When a Congressman wants to propose a new **law**, that person sponsors the **bill** and introduces it to the respective Congressional chamber by either giving it to the clerk or placing it in a special box known as the hopper. A legislative number is assigned to the bill, designated by *H.R.* for bills originating in the House of Representatives or *S.* for bills originating in the Senate. The bill is printed and given to all members of the house. The bill is assigned to a committee for investigation and discussion, which often involves hearings.

Part II

Following an investigation into a proposed bill, the committee releases the bill and recommends that it be passed, recommends that the bill be revised prior to being released, or sets it aside so that it cannot be voted on. If a bill is **released**, it is added to a calendar of bills waiting to be voted on. On the floor of the chamber, the bill is read, and if it passes by a simple majority, it goes to the other congressional house. In order for the bill to be introduced in the other house, a member of that house must **announce the introduction** of it. The same process of being assigned to a committee and investigation is repeated in the second house. If the bill also passes by a simple majority in the second house, it goes to a **conference committee** comprised of members of both houses.

Part III

The **conference committee** reconciles any differences between the two houses with regard to the bill, and if any alterations are made, the committee sends the bill back to each house for final approval. After the bill has been approved, it is **printed**, or **enrolled**, and **certified**. The enrolled bill is then signed by both the Speaker of the House and the Vice President, who is the leader of the Senate. After the bill has received the necessary signatures, it is sent to the President of the United States, where he must sign it within ten days or veto it. If the President **signs** the bill, it becomes law. If the President chooses to **veto** the bill, it is sent back to Congress, and if two-thirds of both houses vote to pass the bill, it becomes law without the President's signature.

Courts of Appeals

The second-highest level of the federal judiciary branch is comprised of the **courts of appeals**. The courts of appeals were created in 1891 to reduce the overwhelming number of cases that were sent to the Supreme Court and more quickly and efficiently process cases. There are twelve **regional**

circuit courts of appeal, as well as the **US Court of Appeals for the Federal Circuit**. Most circuit courts have between ten and fifteen judges, but the number varies widely between courts. The purpose of the courts of appeals is to review the decisions of the district courts or of the trial courts at the federal level, and to review orders of regulatory agencies in instances where the agencies have reviewed the orders themselves internally but there remains dissent over legal issues. The Court of Appeals for the Federal Circuit also has national jurisdiction to hear appeals in unique circumstances.

District Courts

The district courts are below the courts of appeals. There are ninety-four **districts** among the fifty states and territories of the US Districts are established by Congress based on the population, the size, and the caseload in a particular area. Small states can represent an entire district; larger states are divided into up to four districts. There are at minimum two judges for every **district court**. Judges must be residents of the district they work in, with the exception of judges in D.C. District courts sessions are held in varying cities within a district for specific durations of time in each city. The types of cases that appear before district courts address issues related to federal crimes. District courts are the only federal courts in which a grand jury indicts individuals accused of criminal acts and a jury makes a decision on a case. In every district, there is also a **US bankruptcy court**, as bankruptcy issues must be handled in federal courts as opposed to state courts.

Special Courts

Occasionally, a need arises to establish a court to meet a particular purpose. Such special courts are referred to as **legislative courts**, as they are established by Congress. In special courts, judges are appointed to life terms, just as judges are in other federal courts. Also, similarly to other federal court judges, special court judges must be appointed by the President of the US and approved by the Senate. There are currently two special trial courts with national jurisdiction. The first is the **Court of International Trade**, which hears cases dealing with international trade and customs concerns. The second is the **US Court of Federal Claims**, which hears cases involving claims for financial damages against the US government, cases involving disputes concerning federal contracts, cases involving situations in which the federal government is accused of unlawfully taking private property, and other cases involving claims against the US government.

Landmark Supreme Court Cases and Civil Rights

Marbury v. Madison

Right before President **John Adams** left office after **Thomas Jefferson** won the presidency in the election of 1800, he passed the **Judiciary Act of 1801**. This act eliminated one seat on the Supreme Court, eliminated circuit duties for members of the Supreme Court, and created 16 federal circuit court judgeships. This allowed President John Adams to pack the federal court system with his fellow Federalists before Thomas Jefferson, a Democratic-Republican, took office. **William Marbury** was one of these individuals promised a position by John Adams. However, Adams's Secretary of State, **John Marshall**, did not have time to deliver Marbury's commission (which was the formal job offer for Marbury's position as Justice of the Peace for D.C.) before the Jefferson administration took over. The new Secretary of State, **James Madison**, refused to deliver Marbury's commission after he took office. This led to Marbury suing Madison for his commission, and the issue was brought before the Supreme Court in the case of ***Marbury v. Madison*** (1803).

Although Section XIII of the Judiciary Act of 1789 had a **Writ of Mandamus** which required Madison to honor the appointment, Chief Justice **John Marshall**, whom Adams appointed to the Supreme Court before leaving office, declared this section unconstitutional. This historic act established the doctrine of **judicial review**, which allows the Supreme Court to declare a legislative or executive act unconstitutional. Marshall thereby established an independent judiciary; he is quoted as saying, "The Constitution is the supreme Law of the Land, with the Supreme Court as the final interpreter."

McCulloch v. Maryland

When Congress chartered a national bank, the **Second Bank of the United States**, Maryland voted to tax any bank business dealing with banks chartered outside the state, including the federally chartered bank. Andrew McCulloch, an employee of the Second Bank of the US in Baltimore, refused to pay this tax. The resulting lawsuit from the State of Maryland went to the Supreme Court for judgment.

John Marshall, Chief Justice of the Supreme Court, stated that Congress was within its rights to charter a national bank. In addition, the State of Maryland did not have the power to levy a tax on the federal bank or on the federal government in general. In cases where state and federal government collided, precedent was set for the **federal government** to prevail.

The Civil Rights Act of 1871

The Civil Rights Act of 1871 was a statute passed following the Civil War. It was comprised of the **1870 Force Act** and the **1871 Ku Klux Klan Act**, and was passed primarily with the intention of protecting Southern black people from the Ku Klux Klan. Since it was passed in 1871, the statute has only undergone small changes. It has, however, been interpreted widely by the courts. In 1882, some parts of the Civil Rights Act of 1871 were found unconstitutional, but the Force Act and the Klan Act continued to be applied in civil rights cases in subsequent years.

Plessy v. Ferguson

Plessy v. Ferguson was an 1896 Supreme Court case. The case resulted in the decision that **de jure racial segregation** in **public facilities** was legal in the United States, and permitted states to restrict black people from using public facilities. The case originated when, in 1890, a black man named Homer Plessy decided to challenge a Louisiana law that segregated black and white people on trains by sitting in the white section of a train. Plessy was convicted of breaking the law in a Louisiana court, and the case was appealed to the US Supreme Court, where the Supreme Court upheld the Louisiana decision. The case established the legality of the doctrine of separate but equal, thereby allowing racial segregation. The decision was later overturned by **Brown v. the Board of Education of Topeka**.

The Fair Employment Act

The Fair Employment Act was signed by President Franklin Roosevelt in 1941. The purpose of the act was to **ban racial discrimination** in industries related to **national defense**, and it represented the very first federal law to ban discrimination in employment. The **Fair Employment Act** mandated that all federal government agencies and departments concerned with national defense, as well as private defense contractors, guaranteed that professional training would be conducted without discrimination based on race, creed, color, or national origin. The Fair Employment Act was followed by **Title VII of the 1964 Civil Rights Act**, which banned discrimination by private employers, and by **Executive Order 11246** in 1965, which concerned federal contractors and subcontractors.

Brown v. Board of Education

Brown versus the Board of Education of Topeka was a Supreme Court case that was decided in 1954. The case made it illegal for **racial segregation** to exist within **public education facilities**.

This decision was based on the finding that separate but equal public educational facilities would not provide black and white students with the same standard of facilities. The case originated in 1951, when a lawsuit was filed by Topeka parents, who were recruited by the NAACP, against the Board of Education of the City of Topeka, Kansas in a US district court. The parents, one of whom was named Oliver Brown, wanted the Topeka Board of Education to eliminate racial segregation. The district court agreed that segregation had negative effects, but did not force the schools to desegregate because it found that black and white school facilities in the District were generally equal in standards. The case was appealed to the Supreme Court, where the finding was that separate educational facilities are unequal.

Bolling v. Sharpe

Bolling v. Sharpe was a 1954 Supreme Court case. Like Brown v. Board of Education, this case addressed issues concerning **segregation in public schools**. The case originated in 1949, when parents from Anacostia, an area in Washington, DC, petitioned the Board of Education of the District of Columbia to allow all races to attend a new school. The request was denied. A lawsuit was brought before the District Court for the District of Columbia on behalf of a student named Bolling and other students to admit them to the all-white school. The case was dismissed by the district court and taken to the Supreme Court. The Supreme Court ruled that the school had to be desegregated based on the Fifth Amendment.

Civil Rights Act of 1964

The Civil Rights Act of 1964 was passed to protect the rights of both **black men** and **women**. It served as part of the foundation for the women's rights movement. The act was a catalyst for change in the United States, as it made it illegal to engage in acts of **discrimination** in public facilities, in government, and in employment. The Civil Rights Act prohibited unequal voter registration, prohibited discrimination in all public facilities involved in interstate commerce, supported desegregating public schools, ensured equal protection for black people in federally funded programs, and banned employment discrimination.

The Pregnancy Discrimination Act

The Pregnancy Discrimination Act was passed in 1978 as an amendment to the sex discrimination clause of the Civil Rights Act of 1964. The **Pregnancy Discrimination Act** stipulated that people cannot be discriminated against due to pregnancy, childbirth, or medical issues related to pregnancy or childbirth. If a person becomes pregnant, gives birth, or has related medical conditions, they must receive treatment that is equivalent to that received by other employees and also receive equal benefits as other employees. The **Family and Medical Leave Act** was passed in 1993 to advance protections under the Pregnancy Discrimination Act.

Civil Rights Act of 1968

The Civil Rights Act of 1968 was passed following the passing of the Civil Rights Act of 1964. The act made it illegal to **discriminate** against individuals during the sale, rental, or financing of **housing**. Therefore, the act is also referred to as the **Fair Housing Act of 1968**. The act made it illegal to refuse to sell or rent housing based on race, color, religion, or national origin. It also made it illegal to advertise housing for sale or rent and to specify a preference to rent or sell the property to an individual of a particular race, color, religion, or national origin. In addition, the act ensured protection for civil rights workers.

Age Discrimination in Employment Act

The Age Discrimination in Employment Act of 1967 made it illegal for employers to discriminate against people who are **forty years old** or greater in age. The act establishes standards for employer-provided pensions and benefits, and mandates that information regarding the needs of older workers be made publicly available. In addition to generally banning age discrimination, the **ADEA** specifies particular actions that are illegal. Employers may not specify that individuals of a certain age are preferred or are conversely restricted from applying to job ads. Age limits are only permitted to be mentioned in job ads if age has been shown to be a bona fide occupational qualification. The act stipulates that it is illegal to discriminate against age through apprenticeship programs and that it is illegal to restrict benefits to older employees. However, employers are permitted to lower the benefits provided to older employees based on age if the expense of providing fewer or lesser benefits is equivalent to the expense of providing benefits to younger employees.

Loving v. Virginia

Loving v. Virginia was a 1967 Supreme Court case that ruled that a particular law in Virginia known as the **Racial Integrity Act of 1924** was unconstitutional, as the law had prohibited interracial marriage. The Supreme Court ruling would put an end to **race-based restrictions on marriage**. The case originated when Mildred Jeter and Richard Loving, an interracial Virginia couple that was married in Washington, DC due to the Virginia state law prohibiting interracial marriage, returned to Virginia and received charges of violating the interracial marriage ban. After pleading guilty, the couple was forced to move to DC to avoid a jail sentence, where they brought their case to the Supreme Court on the premise that their Fourteenth Amendment rights had been violated. The Supreme Court found that the Virginia law was unconstitutional and overturned the conviction that the couple had been charged with.

Jones v. Mayer

Jones v. Mayer was a 1968 Supreme Court case that ruled that Congress has the authority to **regulate the sale of private property** for the purpose of preventing racial discrimination. This United States Supreme Court ruling was based on a legal statute that stipulates that it is illegal in the United States to commit acts of racial discrimination, both privately and publicly when selling or renting property. The United States Supreme Court ruled that the congressional power to uphold the statute extends from the power of Congress to uphold the Thirteenth Amendment.

Roe v. Wade

Roe v. Wade was a controversial 1973 US Supreme Court case. The case originated in 1970 in Texas, which had an **anti-abortion law**. The plaintiff was an unmarried pregnant woman who was assigned the name "Jane Roe" to protect her identity. Texas anti-abortion law characterized the acts of having or attempting to perform an abortion as crimes, with the exception of cases in which an abortion could save the life of a mother. The lawsuit argued that the Texas law was unconstitutionally vague and was not consistent with the rights guaranteed by the First, Fourth, Fifth, Ninth, and Fourteenth Amendments. While the Texas court ruled in favor of Roe, it did not rule that Texas had to discontinue the enforcement of its anti-abortion law. Roe appealed to the Supreme Court in 1971, and the court's decision in 1973 struck down Texas's abortion laws. The case overturned most state laws prohibiting abortion. In 2022, the supreme court reversed its decision in Roe v Wade, finding no constitutional basis for requiring states to permit abortion, effectively returning the authority to the states to decide.

Regents of the University of California v. Bakke

Regents of the University of California v. Bakke was a 1978 Supreme Court case that banned **quota systems** in the college admissions process but ruled that programs providing **advantages to minorities** are constitutionally sound. The case originated when Allan Bakke, a white male who was a strong student, applied to the University of California at Davis Medical School and was rejected. The school had a program that reserved admissions spots for minority applicants; the program had grown along with the overall size of the school since its opening in 1968. Bakke complained to the school but was still not admitted, and he finally brought his case before the Superior Court of California. The California court ruled in favor of Bakke, who claimed that he had been discriminated against because of his race, and the school appealed to the US Supreme Court. The Supreme Court ruled that race could be used as one factor by discriminatory boards such as college admissions boards; however, quotas were ruled to be **discriminatory**.

Americans with Disabilities Act (ADA)

The ADA was passed by Congress in 1990. This act outlines the rights of individuals with disabilities in society in all ways besides education. It states that they should receive **nondiscriminatory treatment** in jobs, **access** to businesses and other stores, and other services. Due to this law all businesses must be wheelchair accessible, having a ramp that fits the standards of the law, and all doors and bathrooms within those businesses must be able to be used and maneuvered through by someone in a wheelchair. If these rules are not followed, businesses can be subject to large fines until these modifications have been complied with. The ADA also ensures fair treatment when applying for jobs to make sure that there is no unfair discrimination for any person with a disability who is applying to the job.

The Civil Rights Act of 1991

The Civil Rights Act of 1991 is a statute that was passed as a result of a number of Supreme Court decisions that restricted the rights of individuals who had sued their employers on the basis of discrimination. The passing of the **Civil Rights Act of 1991** was the first time since the Civil Rights Act of 1964 was passed that modifications were made to the rights granted under federal laws to individuals in cases involving **employment discrimination**. Specifically, the Civil Rights Act of 1991 granted the right to a trial by jury to individuals involved in cases of employment discrimination, and it also addressed for the first time the potential for emotional distress damages and limited the amount awarded by a jury in such cases.

Planned Parenthood v. Casey

Planned Parenthood of Southeastern Pennsylvania v. Casey was a 1992 Supreme Court case that challenged the constitutionality of Pennsylvania abortion laws. The case was brought before the US District Court for the Eastern District of Pennsylvania by abortion clinics and physicians to challenge four clauses of the **Pennsylvania Abortion Control Act of 1982** as unconstitutional under Roe v. Wade. The district court ruled that all of the clauses of the Pennsylvania act were unconstitutional. The case was then appealed to the Third Circuit Court of Appeals, which ruled to uphold all of the clauses except for one requiring notification of a husband prior to abortion. The case was then appealed to the Supreme Court, which ruled to uphold the constitutional right to have an abortion, thereby upholding Roe v. Wade.

Adarand Constructors, Inc. v. Peña

Adarand Constructors, Inc. v. Peña was a 1995 United States Supreme Court case in which the court ruled that any **racial classifications** that are instituted by representatives of federal, state, or local governments have to be reviewed and analyzed by a court. The court that reviews such racial classifications must abide by a policy of **strict scrutiny**. Strict scrutiny represents the highest standard of Supreme Court review. Racial classifications are deemed constitutional solely under circumstances in which they are being used as specific measures to advance critical and important governmental interests. The ruling of the Supreme Court in this case requiring strict scrutiny as a standard of review for racial classifications overturned the case of **Metro Broadcasting, Inc. v.**

FCC, in which the Supreme Court established a two-level method of reviewing and analyzing racial classifications.

The Employment Non-Discrimination Act (ENDA) and the Equality Act

The Employment Non-Discrimination Act was a proposed United States federal law that was introduced various times before Congress but was never passed by both the House and the Senate. The **Employment Non-Discrimination Act** would ban employers from discriminating against their employees based on their **sexual orientation**. A number of states have already passed laws that ban discrimination based on sexual orientation, including California, Connecticut, Hawaii, Maryland, Massachusetts, Minnesota, Nevada, New Hampshire, New Jersey, New Mexico, New York, Rhode Island, Vermont, and Wisconsin. The ENDA has largely been encompassed by a broader resolution known as the Equality Act, which is a bill that would amend the Civil Rights Act of 1964 to further add gender identity and sexual orientation to the list of prohibited categories of discrimination for employment, public accomodations, the jury system, and housing. It has been met with opposition and has not yet been passed by both bodies of Congress.

Miranda v. Arizona

In 1966, the Supreme Court ruled that law enforcement must warn a person of their constitutional rights before interrogating them. If these rights—known as Miranda rights—are not explained to a person, that person's statements cannot be used as evidence against them at trial. The Supreme Court held that interrogating people without informing of them of their rights is in violation of their Constitutional rights.

In this case, Ernesto Miranda was arrested and charged with the kidnapping and rape of an 18-year-old woman. Miranda was not informed of his right to an attorney or to silence before or during the two-hour long interrogation he was subjected to by the police. The interrogation resulted in both oral and written confessions, which were both brought against Miranda in trial. They were initially accepted as evidence, resulting in Miranda being sentenced for 20-30 years in prison. The conviction was reversed after the Supreme Court's decision, though Miranda was later found guilty of the same crime in a later trial.

Grutter v. Bollinger

Grutter v. Bollinger was a 2003 Supreme Court case that upheld an **affirmative action policy** of the University of Michigan Law School admissions process. The case originated in 1996 when Barbara Grutter, a white in-state resident with a strong academic record, applied to the law school and was denied admission. In 1997, she filed a lawsuit claiming that her rejection was based on racial discrimination and violated her Fourteenth Amendment rights, as well as Title VI of the Civil Rights Act of 1964. The case was heard in 2001 in a US District Court, which ruled that the university's admissions policies were unconstitutional. In 2002, the case was appealed to the Sixth Circuit Court of Appeals, which overturned the lower court's decision. The case was then appealed to the US Supreme Court in 2003, which ruled that the school's affirmative action policy could remain in place, upholding the case of Regents of the University of California v. Bakke permitting race to be a factor in admissions but banning quotas.

Chapter Quiz

Ready to see how well you retained what you just read? Scan the QR code to go directly to the chapter quiz interface for this study guide. If you're using a computer, simply visit the online resources page at **mometrix.com/resources719/clepamergov** and click the Chapter Quizzes link.

Political Parties and Interest Groups

United States Politics

Political Parties

A political party is an organization that advocates a particular ideology and seeks to gain power within government. The tendency of members of political parties to support their party's policies and interests relative to those of other parties is referred to as **partisanship**. Often, a political party is comprised of members whose positions, interests, and perspectives on policies vary, despite having shared interests in the general ideology of the party. As such, many political parties will have divisions within them that have differing opinions on policy. Political parties are often placed on a **political spectrum**, with one end of the spectrum representing conservative, traditional values and policies and the other end of the spectrum representing radical, progressive values and policies.

Types of Party Systems

There is a variety of party systems, including single-party systems, dominant-party systems, and dual-party systems. In a **single-party system**, only one political party may hold power. In this type of system, minor parties may be permitted, but they must accept the leadership of the dominant party. **Dominant-party systems** allow for multiple parties in opposition of one another, but the dominant party is the only party considered to have power. A **two-party system**, such as in the United States, is one in which there are two dominant political parties. In such a system, it is very difficult for any other parties to win an election. In most two-party systems, there is typically one right-wing party and one left-wing party.

Right-Wing Political Parties and Left-Wing Political Parties

Right-wing political parties in the United States of America are typically associated with conservatism or Christian democracy. **Right-wing political parties** and politics are considered to be the opposite of left-wing political parties and politics. In the United States of America, the **Republican Party** is the dominant right-wing political party. **Left-wing political parties** are typically associated with socialism, social democracy, or liberalism. In the United States of America, the **Democratic Party** is the dominant left-wing political party.

Democratic Party

The Democratic Party was founded in 1792. In the United States, it is one of the two dominant political parties, along with the Republican Party. The **Democratic Party** is to the left of the Republican Party. The Democratic Party began as a conservative party in the mid-1800s, shifting to the left during the 1900s. There are many factions within the Democratic Party in the United States. The **Democratic National Committee (DNC)** is the official organization of the Democratic Party, and it develops and promotes the party's platform and coordinates fundraising and election strategies. There are Democratic committees in every US state and most US counties. The official symbol of the Democratic Party is the **donkey**.

Republican Party

The Republican Party is often referred to as the **GOP**, which stands for Grand Old Party. The **Republican Party** is considered socially conservative and economically neoliberal relative to the Democratic Party. Like the Democratic Party, there are factions within the Republic Party that agree with the party's overall ideology but disagree with the party's positions on specific issues.

The official symbol of the Republican Party is the **elephant**. The **Republican National Committee (RNC)** is the official organization of the Republican Party, and it develops and promotes the party's platform and coordinates fundraising and election strategies. There are Republican committees in every US state and most US counties.

POLITICAL CAMPAIGNS

A political campaign is an organized attempt to influence the decisions of a particular group of people. Examples of campaigns could include elections or efforts to influence policy changes. One of the first steps in a campaign is to develop a **campaign message**. The message must then be delivered to the individuals and groups that the campaign is trying to reach and influence through a campaign plan. There are various ways for a campaign to **communicate** its message to the intended audience, including public media; paid media such as television, radio and newspaper ads, billboards, and the internet; public events such as protests and rallies; meetings with speakers; mailings; canvassing; fliers; and websites. Through these efforts, the campaign attempts to attract additional support and, ultimately, to reach the goal of the campaign.

ELEMENTS OF A CAMPAIGN

THE MONEY AND THE MACHINE

Money is a significant aspect of a campaign because with changes in technology, campaigns have become increasingly expensive to run. Some of the costs associated with running a campaign include TV advertisements, mailings, and campaign staff salaries. **Fundraising** is often used to generate money to cover campaign costs. The capital that is necessary to run a campaign refers to human capital, which may consist of paid staff, volunteers, or a combination of both. Key members of a campaign include a campaign manager, people to make strategic decisions, and people to canvass door-to-door and make phone calls.

THE CAMPAIGN MESSAGE

Political campaigns consist of three main elements, which are the campaign message, the money that is necessary to run the campaign and "machine," and the capital that is necessary run the campaign. A campaign message is a succinct statement expressing why voters should support the campaign and the individual or policy associated with that campaign. The message is one of the most significant aspects of a political campaign, and a considerable amount of time, money, and effort is invested in devising a successful campaign message, as it will be repeated throughout the campaign and will be one of the most identifying factors of the campaign.

VOTING

Voting is a method of decision-making that allows people to express their opinion or preference for a candidate or for a proposed resolution of an issue. In a democratic system, **voting** typically takes place as part of an **election**. An individual participates in the voting process by casting a vote, or a **ballot**; ballots are produced by states. A secret ballot can be used at polls to protect voters' privacy. Individuals can also vote via absentee ballot. In some states, voters can write-in a name to cast a vote for a candidate that is not on the ballot. Some states also use straight-ticket voting, allowing the voter to vote for one party for all the elected positions on the ballot.

DIFFERENT VOTING SYSTEMS

Different types of voting systems exist in the United States of America. In a **single-vote system**, the voter can only vote for one option, precluding the voter from voting for anyone else. Alternatively, in a **multiple vote system**, the voter may vote for multiple options. In a **ranked vote system**, a voter may rank alternative options in order of preference. In a **scored, or rated, vote system**, the voter gives each option a score that falls on a scale between one and whatever number represents the upper boundary of the scale.

Voter Eligibility

The United States Constitution establishes that individual people are **permitted to vote** in elections if they are citizens of the United States and are at least eighteen years old. The **fifteenth** and **nineteenth amendments** of the United States Constitution stipulate that the right to vote cannot be denied to any United States citizen based on race or sex, respectively. States regulate voter eligibility beyond the minimum qualifications stipulated by the United States Constitution. Depending on the regulations of individual states, individuals may be denied the right to vote if they are convicted criminals.

Voter Registration

Individuals have the responsibility of **registering to vote**. Every state except North Dakota requires citizens to register to vote. In an effort to increase voter turnout, Congress passed the **National Voter Registration Act** in 1993. The Act is also known as "Motor Voter," because it required states to make the voter registration process easier by providing registration services through drivers' license registration centers, as well as through disability centers, schools, libraries, and mail-in registration. Some states are exempt because they permit same-day voter registration, which enables voters to register to vote on the day of the election.

Elections in the United States

In the United States, officials are **elected** at the federal, state, and local levels. The first two articles of the Constitution, as well as various amendments, establish how **federal elections** are to be held. The President is elected **indirectly** by electors of an electoral college. Members of the electoral college nearly always vote along the lines of the popular vote of their respective states. Members of Congress are **directly** elected. At the state level, state law establishes most aspects of how elections are held. There are many elected offices at the state level, including a governor and state legislature. There are also elected offices at the local level.

Primaries and Caucuses

Candidates for federal office are chosen by primaries and caucuses. In a **primary election**, voters in a jurisdiction choose a political party's candidate for a later election. Candidates for state-level offices are also selected through primaries. The purpose of a **caucus** is also to nominate candidates for a later election. A caucus is a meeting that takes place in a precinct with the purpose of discussing each party's platform and voting issues such as voter turnout. Eleven states hold caucuses. The period of time known as the primary season in Presidential elections, which includes both primaries and caucuses, lasts from the Iowa caucus in January to the last primary, ending in early summer.

Political Media

The political media includes forms of the media that are owned and overseen and managed or influenced by political entities. The purpose of the **political media** is to disseminate the views and platforms of the associated political entity. The media is often referred to as a **fourth power**, in addition to the executive, legislative, and judicial branches of the government. The **internet** has become an additional form of political media. However, the internet is not completely identifiable as a political medium, given the lack of a central authority and the lack of a common political method of communication via the internet.

PETITION

A petition is a request to an authority, most commonly a government official or public office or agency. A **petition** typically takes the form of a document that is addressed to an official who holds authority and that is signed by multiple individuals. In addition to **written petitions**, people may submit **oral petitions**, and today petitions are often internet-based. The First Amendment to the US Constitution contains a clause known as the **Petition Clause**, which guarantees the right "to petition the Government for a redress of grievances." The right to petition includes the right to file lawsuits against the government. Petitions can be used for many purposes. One example includes petitions to qualify candidates for public office to appear on a ballot; in order for a candidate's name to appear on a ballot, the candidate must collect signatures from voters. Other types of petitions include those used in efforts to generate support for various causes.

PROTEST

A protest is an expression of opposition to, and sometimes of support of, events or circumstances. **Protests** represent a means for individuals to publicly make their views heard in an effort to influence public opinion or government policy, or as a means to enact **change**. Protests generally result when self-expression of opposing views is restricted by government policy, political or economic circumstances, religion, social structures, or the media, and people react by declaring their views through cultural mechanisms or on the streets. There are numerous forms of protest, including boycotts, civil disobedience, demonstrations, non-violent protests, picketing, protest marches, protest songs, riots, sit-ins, teach-ins, strikes, and others.

ADVANTAGES AND DISADVANTAGES TO THE TWO-PARTY SYSTEM

Advocates of the two-party system argue that the advantages of such systems are that they are **stable** because they enable policies and government to change slowly rather than rapidly due to the relative lack of influence from small parties representing unconventional ideologies. In addition, they seem to drive voters towards a middle ground and are less susceptible to revolutions, coups, or civil wars. Among the critiques of the two-party system is the claim that stability in and of itself is not necessarily desirable, as it often comes at the expense of **democracy**. Critics also argue that the two-party system promotes negative political campaigns, in which candidates and their respective parties only take positions on issues that will differentiate themselves from their opponents, rather than focusing on policy issues that are of significance to citizens. Another concern is that if one of the two major parties becomes weak, a **dominant-party system** may develop.

CONSTITUTION PARTY

The Constitution Party is a conservative minority party in the US that was originally founded as the US Taxpayers Party in 1992; its name was changed in 1999. The **Constitution Party** represents the third-largest percentage of registered voters in the US. Members believe that US laws originate from the Bible, take a very conservative approach to social issues such as homosexuality and abortion, and push for a more prominent role of religion in the lives of US citizens. Members also support a **stricter conformity** to what they interpret as the original intent of the US Constitution and the principles of the Declaration of Independence. The Constitution Party supports limiting federal government by reducing taxes, regulations, and spending, particularly social programs such as welfare, education, and healthcare. The party is also opposed to US involvement in international affairs, illegal immigration, and governmental welfare, and interprets the Second Amendment as securing the individual right to own guns.

Green Party

The Green Party is a **liberal minority party** that has been in existence since the 1980s. However, it was not until the presidential campaigns of 1996 and 2000, when Ralph Nader ran as the presidential nominee on the **Green Party** ticket, that the party gained widespread recognition. Members of the Green Party have won elections predominantly at the local level in the United States, and typically in nonpartisan-ballot elections where candidates were not identified on the ballot as having an affiliation with a political party. The Green Party advocates decentralization of government and local autonomy. There are ten core values held by the Green Party, which are based on the four pillars of the Green Party in Europe. These are community-based economics, decentralization, ecological wisdom, feminism, grassroots democracy, non-violence, personal and global responsibility, respect for diversity, social justice, and sustainability.

Libertarian Party

The Libertarian Party is a minority party that was created in 1971 out of the belief that the two dominant parties in the US had deviated from the libertarian principles of the American founding fathers. The core value of the **Libertarian Party** is **individual liberty**. The Libertarian Party advocates for a limited government, an end to taxes, a minimally regulated free-market economy, the right to keep and bear arms, drug legalization, abolishment of the government social welfare system, civil liberties, a foreign policy of free trade and non-intervention, and the right to abortion. The party opposes the use of military force to achieve goals, as well as any form of gun control.

Reform Party of the United States of America

The Reform Party of the United States of America is a minority party that was founded in 1995 by Ross Perot out of the belief that US citizens were disillusioned with politics and wanted an **alternative** to the two dominant parties. Some of the issues that formed the platform of the **Reform Party** were financial reform issues, including the federal deficit and national debt; government reform issues such as term limits, campaign finance reform, and lobbying reform; and trade issues. The Reform Party advocates maintaining a balanced budget, campaign finance reform, responsible immigration enforcement, opposition to free trade agreements like NAFTA, withdrawal from the WTO, limiting social welfare programs, and term limits for US Representatives and Senators.

Modern Election Campaigns in the United States

Political campaigns in the US have changed and continue to change as advances in technology permit varied campaign methods. Campaigns represent a **civic practice**, and today they are a high-profit industry. The US has an abundance of **professional political consultants** that employ highly sophisticated campaign management strategies and tools. The election process varies widely between the federal, state, and local levels. Campaigns are typically controlled by individual candidates rather than by the parties that they are associated with. Larger campaigns utilize a vast array of media to reach their targeted audiences, while smaller campaigns are typically limited to direct contact with voters, direct mailings, and other forms of low-cost advertising to reach their audiences. In addition to fundraising and spending done by individual candidates, party committees and political action committees also raise money and spend it in ways that will advance the cause of the particular campaign they are associated with.

Canvassing

Canvassing is a method used to solicit votes from people that enables a political campaign to speak with a large number of individuals. The goals of **canvassing** efforts are to try to convince voters to vote for a candidate, to increase recognition of a candidate's name, and to generate supporters.

Canvassing can take one of two forms: field canvassing and phone canvassing. **Field canvassing** is done door to door, approaching every residence in a voting district. This method typically enables canvassers to speak with an increased number of people, who are generally more inclined to speak with someone in person than over the phone, and also enables canvassers to distribute literature and put up lawn signs. Sometimes, the candidate will also conduct field canvassing efforts. **Phone canvassing** is typically done using a phone bank, and therefore can reach even more people than field canvassing efforts. Phone canvassing is particularly useful in rural areas. However, many individuals are not receptive to unsolicited phone calls, which they associate with telemarketing.

Political Campaign Staff

The staff employed by a political campaign receive a salary in exchange for their efforts to devise and implement a strategy for a successful campaign. Campaigns are typically led by a **campaign manager**. Beneath the campaign manager are **department directors**. The various departments in a political campaign can include the field department, the communications department, the finance department, the compliance and legal departments, the technology department, and the scheduling and advance department, which sends people to events in advance of a candidate to ensure that the details of the event are in order. Beneath the department level, campaign structure varies widely. On larger campaigns, there may be multiple **coordinators**, each serving a particular function within individual departments. **Interns** and **volunteers** represent the bottom tier of the campaign, and they perform the necessary but tedious tasks of the campaign.

Presidential Elections

The President of the United States is elected **indirectly** by members of an **electoral college**. Members of the electoral college nearly always vote along the lines of the popular vote of their respective states. The winner of a presidential election is the candidate with at least 270 **Electoral College votes**. It is possible for a candidate to win the electoral vote and lose the popular vote. Incumbent Presidents and challengers typically prefer a balanced ticket, where the President and Vice President are elected together and generally balance one another with regard to geography, ideology, or experience working in government. The nominated Vice Presidential candidate is referred to as the President's **running mate**.

Electoral College

Electoral college votes are cast by state by a group of electors; each elector casts one **electoral college vote**. State law regulates how states cast their electoral college votes. In all states except Maine and Nebraska, the candidate winning the most votes receives all of the state's electoral college votes. In Maine and Nebraska, two electoral votes are awarded based on the winner of the statewide election, and the rest go to the highest vote-winner in each of the state's congressional districts. Critics of the electoral college argue that it is undemocratic because the President is elected **indirectly** as opposed to directly, and that it creates inequality between voters in different states because candidates focus attention on voters in swing states who could influence election results. Critics argue that the electoral college provides more representation for voters in small states than large states, where more voters are represented by a single electoral than in small states, and discriminates against candidates that do not have support concentrated in a given state.

Congressional Elections

Congressional elections are every two years. Members of the **House of Representatives** are elected for a two-year term, and elections occur every two years on the first Tuesday after November 1st in even years. A Representative is elected from each of 435 House districts in the US. House elections usually occur in the same year as Presidential elections. Members of the **Senate** are elected to six-year terms; one-third of the Senate is elected every two years. Per the

Seventeenth Amendment to the Constitution, which was passed in 1913, Senators are elected by the electorate of states. The country is divided into Congressional districts, and critics argue that this division eliminates voter choice, sometimes creating areas in which Congressional races are uncontested. Every ten years, **redistricting** of Congressional districts occurs. However, redistricting is often partisan and therefore reduces the number of competitive districts. The division of voting districts resulting in an unfair advantage to one party in elections is known as **gerrymandering**. Gerrymandering has been criticized as being undemocratic.

State and Local Elections

State elections are regulated by state laws and constitutions. In keeping with the ideal of separation of powers, the legislature and the executive are elected separately at the **state** level, as they are at the federal level. In each state, a governor and a lieutenant governor are elected. In some states, the Governor and Lieutenant Governor are elected on a joint ticket, while in other states, they are elected separately from one another. In some states, executive positions such as Attorney General and Secretary of State are also elected offices. All members of state legislatures are elected, including state senators and state representatives. Depending on the state, members of the state supreme court and other members of the state judiciary may be chosen in elections. **Local government** can include the governments of counties and cities. At this level, nearly all government offices are filled through an election process. Elected local offices may include sheriffs, county school boards, and city mayors.

Campaign Finance

Hard vs. Soft Money

Running a campaign requires money; however, the means of funding campaigns is often controversial. Both individuals and organizations donate significant private contributions to campaigns. Money donated to campaigns can be characterized as either hard money or soft money. **Hard money** is contributed directly to a campaign. **Soft money** is not contributed directly to a campaign and is not legally coordinated by the official campaign itself; it is, however, spent to fund efforts that benefit the candidate, such as advertising. The administration and enforcement of campaign finance law is the responsibility of the Federal Election Commission, which was created in 1975.

Disclosure

Campaign finance law mandates that candidate committees, party committees, and PACs must file reports **disclosing** the money that they fundraise and spend. Federal candidate committees must disclose all PACs and party committees that donate money to them; the names, occupations, employers, and addresses of all individuals who donate more than $200 in an election cycle; and all expenditures greater than $200 per election cycle for services rendered by an individual or vendor. States and local candidates are also mandated to disclose donations from PACs and party committees. It is becoming commonplace for campaign finance statements to be filed electronically.

Independent Expenditures

An individual or group is legally permitted to make unlimited **independent expenditures** in association with federal elections. An independent expenditure is an expenditure that is made to pay for a form of **communication** that supports the election or defeat of a candidate; the expenditure must be made independently from the candidate's own campaign. To be considered independent, the communication may not be made with the cooperation or consultation with, or at the request or suggestion of, any candidate, any committees or political party associated with the candidate, or any agent that acts on behalf of the candidate. There are no restrictions on the amount that anyone may spend on an independent expenditure; however, any individual making an independent expenditure must report it and disclose the source of the funds they used.

Activities of Political Parties

Political parties participate in federal elections at the local, state, and national levels. Most party committees must register with the **Federal Election Committee** and file reports disclosing federal campaign activities. While party committees may contribute funds directly to federal candidates, the amounts that they contribute are restricted by the campaign finance contribution limits. National and state party committees are permitted to make additional coordinated expenditures, within limits, to assist their nominees in general elections. However, national party committees are not permitted to make unlimited independent expenditures to support or oppose federal candidates using **soft money**. State and local party committees are also not permitted to use soft money for the purpose of supporting or opposing federal candidates, but they are allowed to spend soft money, up to a limit of $10,000 per source, on voter registration and on efforts aimed at increasing voter participation. All party committees are required to **register** themselves and **file disclosure reports** with the Federal Election Committee once their federal election activities exceed specified monetary limits.

Campaign Finance Reform

Reform Through the Federal Election Campaign Act

In 1974, Congress passed the Federal Election Campaign Act, requiring candidates to disclose sources of campaign contributions and expenditures. The act was amended to **limit campaign contributions**. The act limited individual contributions to $1,000 per campaign, banned direct contributions from corporations and trade unions, and limited contributions from **political action committees**, known as **PACs**, to $5,000 per campaign. A PAC is a private group that is organized on behalf of a special interest to aid in efforts to elect or defeat political candidates; the overriding goal of a PAC is to support candidates who would further legislation that is in the interest of the special interest. The number of PACs in the US exceeds 4,000 due to the increase in the creation of PACs in response to the ban on campaign contributions from corporations and trade unions. The **Federal Election Campaign Act** introduced public funding for Presidential primaries and elections and called for the creation of the **Federal Election Committee**, which administers campaign finance law.

Reform Through the Bipartisan Reform Act

In 2002, Congress passed the Bipartisan Campaign Reform Act. The act made it illegal for local and national parties to spend soft money and for national party committees to accept or spend soft money, it increased the limit placed on individual campaign contributions from $1,000 to $2,000, it banned corporations or trade unions from contributing to issue advertising directly, and it made it illegal for corporations or trade unions to fund advertisements that mention a federal candidate within 60 days of a general election or within 30 days of a primary.

Front Loading and Invisible Primaries

Sometimes, too many primaries take place early in the primary season, resulting in a reduction in the number of realistic Presidential candidates because campaign donors withdraw their support for those candidates that are not viewed as viable options; this is called **front loading**. The candidates that are most successful in their run for office are not always the candidates who do well in the early primaries. Some candidates attempt to generate support, funding, and media coverage prior to the start of the official primaries in what is referred to as the **invisible primaries**.

Public Opinion

Public opinion represents the collective attitudes of individual members of the adult population in the United States of America. There are many varied forces that may influence **public opinion**. These forces include public relations efforts on the part of political campaigns and political parties. Another force affecting political opinion is the political media and the mass media. Public opinion is very important during elections, particularly Presidential elections, as it is an indicator of how candidates are perceived by the public and of how well candidates are doing during their election campaigns. Public opinion is often measured and evaluated using **survey sampling**.

Mass Media and Public Opinion

The mass media is critical in developing **public opinion**. In the short term, people generally evaluate information they receive relative to their own beliefs; in the long term, the media may have a considerable impact on people's beliefs. Due to the impact of the media on an individual's beliefs, some experts consider the effects of the media on an individual's independence and autonomy to be negative. Others view the impact of the media on individuals as a positive one, because the media provides information that expands worldviews and enriches life, and fosters the development of opinions that are informed by many sources of information. A critical aspect of the relationship between the media and public opinion is who is in control of the knowledge and information that is disseminated through the media. Whoever controls the media can propagate their own agenda. The extent to which an individual interprets and evaluates information received through the media can influence behaviors such as voting patterns or consumer behavior, as well as social attitudes.

Survey Sampling

Survey sampling is a method that involves the random selection of a sample from a population that is fixed in size. Survey sampling is often used to measure public opinion. The simplest method of **survey sampling** is referred to as **simple random sampling**. Simple random sampling makes sure that each and every possible subset of the defined population which has the desired sample size is given the same probability of being selected. Another method of survey sampling is **stratified sampling**. In addition, **cluster sampling** and **multistage sampling** represent other methods of survey sampling.

Special Interest Groups

A special interest group is a political organization that is created to influence policy or legislators involved in a particular policy area. **Special interest groups** could include corporations, trade associations, trade unions, senior citizens or individuals with disabilities, or even groups within the legislature or bureaucracy. The goal of special interest groups is to attempt to influence government. There are two types of special interest groups: protective groups and promotional groups. **Protective groups** represent one part of society, such as professional organizations, veterans' organizations, and trade unions. Membership in protective groups is limited to individuals who are members of the organizations representing the specific part of society they do. In contrast, **promotional groups** advocate a greater cause and claim to represent the common interests of humankind. Examples of promotional groups include Greenpeace and Friends of the Earth. Membership in promotional groups is open to all individuals, and, as such, are much larger than protective groups.

United States Political Ideologies

Liberalism

Liberalism is an ideology based on the **autonomy** of individuals. **Liberalism** favors civil and political liberties and seeks to maximize those liberties under law and ensure protection from arbitrary authority. A system characterized by liberalism would possess a pluralistic liberal democratic system of government, a rule of law, the free exchange of ideas, and economic competition. The basic **principles of liberalism** include transparency; individual and civil rights, particularly the right to life, liberty, and property, equal rights for all citizens under law; and government by the consent of the governed, which is guaranteed through elections. Liberalism also favors laissez-faire economics, the free market, and the gold standard.

Libertarianism

Libertarianism is an ideology that seeks to maximize **individual rights**, **private property rights**, and **free-market capitalism**. Individuals who subscribe to the ideology of **libertarianism** believe that people should have the freedom to do what they will with their bodies and their private property as long as they do not coerce others to do the same. They also believe that individuals should have the liberty to make their own moral choices, as long as they do not use coercion to prevent others from exercising the same liberty, and that government should not prevent an individual from making a moral choice or impose moral obligations on people. Libertarians advocate minimum government involvement except to protect liberty and prevent coercion. In addition, libertarians support capitalism, oppose social welfare, and oppose government spending and programming that is not aimed at protecting liberty.

American Liberalism

American liberalism is a political ideology that is derived from classical liberalism. Like classical liberalism, **American liberalism** is defined by the ideal of **individual liberty**. However, American liberalism typically rejects laissez-faire economics and instead advocates for the creation and maintenance of institutions that foster **social and economic equity**. American liberalism began in the beginning of the 20th century and started to decline in the 1970s. American liberalism features support for government social programs, increased funding for public education, labor unions, regulation of business, civil rights, voting rights, reproductive rights, strong environmental regulations, public transportation, minimum wage requirements, government funding to alternative energy research, animal rights, gun control, and a progressive tax system. People who subscribe to American liberalism oppose the death penalty.

Nationalism

Nationalism is an ideology based upon the ideal that **identification with a nation, ethnicity, or nationalit**y is an essential and defining part of human social existence. **Nationalism** is thus a universal ideology. However, nationalism also refers to the ideology that one national identity is superior to others and to the view that nations benefit from acting independently rather than collectively. This view of nationalism often spawns nationalist movements, which make political claims on behalf of particular nations. Nationalists differentiate between nations based on specific criteria and also differentiate between individual people based on which nation they are a member of. The criteria used to define national identity include ethnicity, a common language, a common culture, and common values. Nationalism has had an extremely significant impact on world history and geopolitics since the **nation-state** has become the prevailing form of state. Most people in the world currently live in states which are nation-states.

Review Video: American Nationalism
Visit mometrix.com/academy and enter code: 865693

Review Video: Historical Nationalism
Visit mometrix.com/academy and enter code: 510185

Conservatism

Conservatism is a political ideology that is founded on **traditional values**, a **distrust of government,** and **resistance to changes** in the established social order. Most **conservative** political parties are right-wing, but some countries do have conservative political parties that are left-wing. All conservatives place a high value on tradition, which refers to standards and institutions that have been demonstrated to foster good. Conservatives view traditional values as authoritative and judge the world by the standards they have come to believe in, including a belief in God. Conservatives consider tradition to be above the political process. They also disagree with the laws and constitutions of liberal democracies that allow behavior that is in opposition to traditional values. Conservatives in a democracy opt to participate, separate, or resist. Participation on the part of conservatives in a democracy usually takes the form of liberal republican politics, in which conservatives use government policy to promote their values. The imposition of conservative values on the public is typical of nationalist or religious conservatives.

Green Politics

Green politics is a political ideology based on **environmentalism** and **sustainability**. It is seen as an alternative to both left- and right-wing views, and individuals identifying themselves with the left or right tend to view **green politics** as distinct from their own ideology. As a movement, green politics typically grows at a slow rate but does not readily lose support to other views or parties over time. Some of the features of green politics include support of consensus decision making, participatory democracy, and deliberative democracy; green taxes; alternative measures of economic growth; opposition to the subsidy of pollution by government; opposition to nuclear power, persistent organic pollutants, and biological forms of pollution; investing in human capital; accounting reform; an end to the War on Drugs in the United States and Europe; an end to the War on Terrorism; and the curtailment of civil rights.

Pacifism

Pacifism is an ideology that is based on **opposition to war**. **Pacifism** varies from a preference for the use of non-military means in resolving disputes to complete opposition to the use of violence or force in any situation. Pacifism may be based on principle or pragmatism. Pacifism based on principle is founded on the belief that war, violence, force, and coercion are morally wrong. Pacifism based on pragmatism is founded on the belief that there are more preferable means of resolving disputes than war, and that the costs of war outweigh the benefits. An individual who opposes war is often referred to as a **dove** or as being dovish, alluding to the peaceful nature of the dove.

Republicanism

Republicanism is a political ideology founded on the concept of a nation being governed by an **elected representative** rather than a monarch. Today, the elected representative is most often referred to as the President. A **republic** is a state in which sovereignty resides with the people, as well as a political system in which individual liberty is protected through the power of citizens to elect representatives. These representatives are responsible to the citizens who elected them, and govern according to law. **Republicanism** also represents the ideologies of the political parties that identify themselves as the Republican Party.

Feminism

Feminism is an ideology founded on the belief that there should be **social, political, and economic equality** between the sexes. This belief has manifested itself in a social movement known as the **feminist movement**, which advocates equal rights for women. As such, feminism typically focuses on issues that pertain to women, such as reproductive rights, domestic violence, maternity leave, equal pay, sexual harassment, sexual discrimination, and sexual violence, as well as on the themes of patriarchy, stereotyping, objectification, and oppression. In the 1960s and '70s, feminism focused on issues faced by Western, white, middle-class women while claiming to represent all women. Feminism has since progressed to focus on the connection between gender and sexuality with other social factors, such as race and class. Modern feminism addresses issues that cross class, racial, cultural, and religious boundaries, as well as issues that are specific and pertinent to individual cultures. Feminism also addresses whether particular issues associated with women, such as rape, incest, and mothering, are universal issues.

Chapter Quiz

Ready to see how well you retained what you just read? Scan the QR code to go directly to the chapter quiz interface for this study guide. If you're using a computer, simply visit the online resources page at **mometrix.com/resources719/clepamergov** and click the Chapter Quizzes link.

Political Beliefs and Behavior

Governing Systems

REPRESENTATIVE DEMOCRACY

In a system of government characterized as a **representative democracy**, voters elect representatives to act in their interests. Typically, a **representative** is elected by and responsible to a specific subset of the total population of eligible voters; this subset of the electorate is referred to as a representative's **constituency**. A representative democracy may foster a more powerful legislature than other forms of government systems; to compensate for a strong legislature, most constitutions stipulate that measures must be taken to balance the powers within government, such as the creation of a separate judicial branch. Representative democracy became popular in postindustrial nations where increasing numbers of people expressed an interest in politics but where technology and census counts remained incompatible with systems of direct democracy. Today, the majority of the world's population resides in representative democracies, including constitutional monarchies that possess a strong representative branch.

ANARCHISM

Anarchism is a philosophy that is synonymous with **anti-authoritarianism**. Many people wrongly associate anarchism with chaos, but in fact, anarchists embrace political philosophies and social movements that support the abolition of government and social hierarchy. In a system that is based on **anarchism**, political and economic institutions would not exist. Rather, individual and community relationships would be voluntary, and people would strive towards a society based on autonomy and freedom. On the one hand, anarchists oppose coercive institutions and social hierarchies, and on the other, they advocate a positive conception of how a voluntary society could work. As with many political ideologies, there are many factions that fall under the umbrella of anarchism that hold varying opinions of how anarchism should be defined. For instance, some anarchists support the use of violence to promote their ideology, while others do not.

AUTHORITARIANISM

Authoritarian regimes enforce strong, even oppressive, measures against individuals that fall within their sphere of influence; they often arise when a governing body presumes that it knows what is right for a nation and enforces it. They are typically led by an elite group that employs repressive measures to maintain power, and they do not generally make efforts to gain the consent of individuals or permit feedback on their policies. Under an **authoritarian** government, people are often subject to **government control** over aspects of their lives that in many other systems would be considered personal matters. There is a spectrum of authoritarian ideologies. Examples of authoritarian regimes include absolute monarchies and dictatorships. Democracies can also exhibit authoritarian characteristics in some situations, such as efforts to promote national security. Authoritarian governments typically extend broad-reaching powers to law enforcement bodies, sometimes resulting in a police state; they may or may not have a rule of law and are often corrupt.

TOTALITARIANISM

Totalitarianism is a form of authoritarian political system in which the government **regulates** practically every aspect of public and private conduct. Under **totalitarianism**, individuals and institutions are enveloped into the state's ideology, and the government imposes its political authority by exercising absolute and centralized control over all aspects of life. Individuals are subordinate to the state, and opposition to political and cultural expression is suppressed.

Totalitarian regimes do not tolerate activities by individuals or groups that are not geared toward achieving the state's goals and maintaining the state's ideology. A totalitarian regime maintains power via the use of secret police, propaganda disseminated through government-controlled media, regulation and restriction of free speech, and the use of terror tactics.

Communism

Communism is a form of an authoritarian, or in some cases totalitarian, political system. A communist country is governed by a single political party that upholds the principles of **Marxism-Leninism**. The goal of communism is to dissolve the state into a **classless society**. According to Marxism, a communist state is one in which the resources and means of production are communally owned rather than individually owned and which provides for equal sharing of all freedoms, work, and benefits. Marxism argues that socialism is a necessary intermediate phase in achieving communism. Therefore, states that are governed by a communist party are actually socialist states and not true communist states, since a true communist state could not exist given the goal of elimination of the state. Historically, communist states have often arisen during political instability. Within communist states, there have rarely been restrictions on state power, resulting in state structures that are totalitarian or authoritarian. Marxist-Leninist ideology views any restriction on state power as an interference in the goal of reaching communism.

Fascism

Fascism is an authoritarian political ideology and defined the form of rule in Italy from 1922 to 1943 under the leadership of **Mussolini**. Fascism is characterized by efforts to exert state control over all aspects of life, to hold the nation and political party above the individual, and to hold the state as supreme. Fascism also emphasizes loyalty to a single leader and submission to a single nationalistic culture. Fascists support **corporatism** as an economic system, in which economic and social interests of diverse individuals are combined with the interests of the state.

Autocracy, Absolutism, Despotism, and Dictatorship

Autocracy is a form of a political system in which unlimited power is held by a single person. **Absolutism** is a form of autocratic political system. Absolutists believe that one person should hold all power. Historically, a monarch ruled in a system characterized as absolutist. Some people believed that an absolute ruler was chosen by God; in this case, opposition against the monarch was equivalent to opposition to God. Therefore, rule was considered absolute in the sense that the ruler could not be challenged. **Despotism** is another form of autocratic political system, characterized as having a government overseen by a single authority that wields absolute power; the authority could be either an individual or a group. A **dictatorship** is a form of absolute rule by a leader, referred to as a dictator, who is unrestricted by law, constitutions, or other social and political forces. Dictatorships are typically associated with single-party states, military regimes, and other forms of authoritarianism.

Monarchy

Monarchy is one of the oldest forms of government and is defined as an autocratic system in which a monarch serves as **Head of State**. In such a system, the monarch holds office for life. Also included in a monarchy are the individuals and institutions that comprise the royal establishment. In **elective monarchies**, monarchs are appointed to their position for life; in most instances, elective monarchies have been succeeded by **hereditary monarchies**. In a hereditary monarchy, the title of monarch is inherited according to a line of succession; typically one family can trace its origin along a dynasty or bloodline. Most monarchs represent merely a symbol of continuity and statehood, rather than actually serving as a participant in partisan politics. The practice of choosing a monarch varies between countries. A **constitutional monarchy** is one in which the rule of succession is typically established by a law passed by a representative body.

Patriarchy and Tyranny

A patriarchy is a form of autocratic system in which the male members of society tend to hold positions of power. In such a system, the more powerful a position is, the more likely it is that a male will hold that position. **Patriarchy** also describes systems that are characterized as having male leadership in certain hierarchical churches or religious bodies. **Tyranny** is also a form of autocratic system, in which an individual described as a tyrant possesses and wields absolute power and rules by tyranny. Tyrants are typically characterized as cruel despots that place greater significance on their own interests or the interests of a small group of individuals than on the interests of the population and the state that they govern.

Democracy

Democracy, or **rule by the people**, is a form of government in which power is vested in the people and in which policy decisions are made by the majority in a decision-making process such as an election that is open to all or most citizens. Definitions of democracy have become more generalized and include aspects of society and political culture in democratic societies that do not necessarily represent a form of government. What defines a democracy varies, but some of the characteristics of a democracy could include the presence of a middle class, the presence of a civil society, a free market, political pluralism, universal suffrage, and specific rights and freedoms. In practice, however, democracies do have limits on specific freedoms, which are justified as being necessary to maintain democracy and ensure democratic freedoms. For example, freedom of association is limited in democracies for individuals and groups that pose a threat to government or to society.

Parliamentary System

A parliamentary system is a representative democratic system in which the executive branch of government is dependent on the support of a **parliament**. In this system, there is no obvious separation of powers between the executive and legislative branches. However, **parliamentary systems** are generally flexible and responsive to the public. They are characterized as having both a head of government, who is typically the prime minister, and a head of state, who is often a symbol possessing only ceremonial powers. Some parliamentary systems also have an elected president. The features of a parliamentary system include an executive cabinet, headed by the head of government. The cabinet can be removed by the parliament by a vote of no confidence, and likewise, the parliament can be dissolved by the executive.

Presidential/Congressional System

In a presidential system, also referred to as a **congressional system**, the legislative branch and the executive branch are elected separately. The features of a **presidential system** include a president who serves as both the head of state and the head of the government, who has no formal relationship with the legislative branch, who is not a voting member, who cannot introduce bills, and who has a fixed term of office. Elections are held at scheduled times. The president's cabinet carries out the policies of the executive branch and the legislative branch.

Oligarchy

Oligarchy, or **rule by the few**, is a form of political system in which the majority of political power is held by a small portion of society. This power usually resides with the most powerful individuals or groups, such as those that possess wealth, military might, or political influence. Oftentimes, **oligarchies** are comprised of a few powerful families, in which power is passed on from one generation to the next. Members of oligarchies may not wield their power openly but may instead exercise power from behind the scenes, particularly through economic measures.

Aristocracy, Meritocracy, and Plutocracy

Aristocracy is a form of oligarchic system in which the government is led by a ruling class that is considered, either by themselves or by others, to be superior to other members of society. **Meritocracy**, or rule by those who most deserve to rule, is a system that is more flexible than an aristocracy. In a meritocracy, rulers are not automatically considered the best rulers for life but must demonstrate their abilities and achievements in order to maintain power. A **plutocracy** is a system of government led by the wealthy. There is often an overlap between the classification of a government as an aristocracy and a plutocracy, because wealth can enable individuals to portray their own qualities and merits as the best.

A Republic

A republic is a state in which supreme power rests with **citizens** who vote to elect representatives to be responsible to them. The organization of government in a **republic** can vary. In most republics, the head of state is referred to as the president, and in a democratic republic, the head of state is chosen in an election. In some countries, the constitution restricts the number of terms that an individual can serve as president. In the United States, where the head of state is also the head of government, the system is known as a **presidential system**.

Federal Republic

A federal republic is a state that defines itself as both a federation and a republic. A **federation** is a state that is made up of multiple self-governing regions that are united by a central, federal government. The self-government of independent states is guaranteed by a constitution and is not able to be repealed by the central government. Three countries currently characterize themselves as **federal republics**: the Federal Republic of Germany, the Federal Republic of Nigeria, and the Federal Democratic Republic of Ethiopia.

Commonwealth

A commonwealth is a state that is founded on law and united by a compact or by an agreement made by its citizens for the common good of the entire state and for the citizens of the state. In a **commonwealth**, supreme authority is held by the **people**. In the United States, the state of Kentucky, the state of Massachusetts, the state of Pennsylvania, and the state of Virginia are all classified as commonwealths. The term *commonwealth* is also used to describe Puerto Rico and the Northern Marianas Islands, which are both self-governing, autonomous political units that voluntarily associate themselves with the United States of America.

Socialist Republic

In a socialist republic, the constitution or other political doctrine stipulates that the republic operates under a **socialist economic system**, such as a Marxist system. Some **socialist republics** are under the power of a party whose platform is founded on communist ideology, and as such, are referred to as communist states by Western nations. Examples of republics that use the term socialist in their names include the Democratic Socialist Republic of Sri Lanka and the Socialist Republic of Vietnam. Some countries that define themselves as socialist republics, such as India and Guyana, do so in their constitutions rather than in their names. Other countries that identify themselves as socialist republics include North Korea, the People's Republic of China, and Cuba.

THEOCRACY

A theocracy is a form of a government system in which **religion** or **faith** plays a significant role in the way that the government is run. Commonly, in countries that identify themselves as a **theocracy**, civil rulers are also the leaders of the dominant religion. In these countries, government policies are often strongly guided by religion. Usually, a theocratic government makes a claim to rule on behalf of God or another higher power. The administrative hierarchy of the government often serves as the administrative hierarchy of the dominant religion as well.

TRIBALISM

Tribalism was the first social system that humans created and coexisted in. It is a system in which society is divided into relatively independent groups referred to as **tribes**. In such a society, tribes themselves have some level of organizational structure, but there is generally very little organization between tribes. Tribes are typically characterized by simple internal organization and structure, with very few differences in social status between individuals. Some tribes nurture the belief that all individuals are equal, and many tribes do not embrace the concept of private property.

ECONOMIC SYSTEM

An economic system addresses the production, distribution, and consumption of goods and services within society and focuses on solving the economic problems of the allocation and scarcity of resources. The composition of an **economic system** consists of people and institutions and the relationships between them. The three questions that must be answered in an economic system are 1) **what** to produce, 2) **how** to produce it, and 3) **for whom** to produce. There are many different types of economic systems, which are often associated with particular ideologies and political systems. Examples of economic systems include market economies, mixed economies, planned economies, traditional economies, and participatory economies.

CAPITALISM

Capitalism is an economic system in which the means of production are **privately owned**; in which the investment of capital, and the production, distribution and prices of goods and services are determined in a **free market**; and in which the goal of production is to generate **profits**. The features of a **capitalist economic system** include a private sector, private property, free enterprise, and profit. Other features of a capitalist economic system include unequal distribution of wealth, competition, self-organization, the existence of markets, the existence of both a bourgeoisie class and a proletariat class, and the pursuit of self-interest.

FEUDALISM

Feudalism is a political and economic system that was in existence in Europe from the 9th century through the 15th century. **Feudalism** in the Medieval Age was based on the relationships between lords and vassals and fiefs. A **lord** was a person who held a title of nobility and who owned land. A **vassal** was an individual who was loaned a piece of land by a lord. The piece of land that was owned by the lord and loaned to the vassal was referred to as a **fief**. In exchange for being loaned the fief, the vassal provided military service to the lord.

SOCIALISM

Socialism refers to an economic system in which the means of production and the distribution of goods and services are owned **collectively** or are owned by a **centralized government** that often plans and controls the economy. In practice, **socialism** also refers to the economic phase in **Marxist-Leninist theory** that falls somewhere between capitalism and communism, in which collective ownership of the economy by the proletariat, or the working class, has not yet been achieved. The goal of a socialist economic system is to achieve collective ownership and, ultimately, to achieve a **classless society**.

Mixed Economy

A mixed economy is an economic system blending capitalism and socialism. Such a system is characterized by both private economic freedom and by centralized economic planning. The majority of Western countries, including the United States, have a **mixed economy**. Features of a mixed economy include the freedoms to possess means of production, to travel, to buy and sell, to hire and fire, to organize labor unions or associations, the freedom of communication, and the freedom to protest peacefully. In addition, mixed economies typically provide legal assistance, libraries, roads, schools, hospitals, protection of person and property both at home and abroad, subsidies to agriculture and other businesses, and government monopolies and government-granted monopolies, all of which are funded by taxes or subsidies. There are provisions for autonomy over personal finances, but mixed economies also include socially oriented involuntary spending programs such as welfare, social security, and government subsidies for businesses. Mixed economies also impose environmental, labor, consumer, antitrust, intellectual property, corporate, and import and export laws, as well as taxes and fees.

Colonialism and Imperialism

Colonialism is a political and economic system that is defined as the extension of a nation's sovereignty over territory and people outside its own boundaries, often amounting to the exploitation of a weaker country by a relatively stronger country. Most often, the stronger country is interested in the use of the weaker country's resources, including labor, to strengthen and enrich itself. **Colonialism** also refers to the set of beliefs and values that is used to validate and advance this system, particularly the belief that the culture and civilization of the relatively stronger colonizing country are superior to those of the relatively weaker colonized country. **Imperialism** is a policy of extending control or authority over foreign countries via territorial acquisition or by the establishment of economic and political control over other countries.

Review Video: An Overview of American Imperialism
Visit mometrix.com/academy and enter code: 629170

Neocolonialism

Neocolonialism is a political and economic system in which a **powerful country** uses economic and political measures to extend or continue its influence over **less developed countries**. The term was devised to describe circumstances at the international level after the fall of European colonial empires in the 19th and 20th centuries, particularly the phenomenon of countries and multinational corporations seeking control over other countries through indirect means, such as economic policies, as opposed to the direct military-political control that traditional colonial powers sought. Many people argue that economic tools, such as restrictions on trade and embargos, that are employed by stronger, more developed countries in their relations with less developed countries are reminiscent of colonial power.

Command/Planned Economy

A planned economy is an economic system in which decisions about the production, allocation, and consumption of goods and services are planned in advance; planning can be carried out in either a centralized or decentralized approach. In most **planned economies**, the plans are carried out by means of commands; therefore, planned economies are also commonly referred to as **command economies**. An economic system that is centrally planned by a government is generally referred to as economic statism. Economic statism, by definition, is the practice of giving a centralized government control over economic planning and policy.

Nazism

Nazism was the ideology of the National Socialist German Workers Party (which was led by **Adolf Hitler** in Nazi Germany from 1933 to 1945) during the **Third Reich**. Followers of **Nazism** believed that the Aryan race was superior to other races, and promoted Germanic racial supremacy and a strong, centrally governed state. Nazism is illegal in modern Germany, but small factions of Neo-Nazis continue to exist both in Germany and abroad. Nazis believed that military power would produce a strong nation, opposed multilingualism and multiculturalism, and sought the unification of all German-speaking individuals. Qualities of Nazism included racism; anti-Semitism; the desire for the creation of a master race; anti-Slavism; the belief in the superiority of the White, Germanic, Aryan, or Nordic races; anti-Marxism, anti-Communism, and anti-Bolshevism; rejection of democracy; social Darwinism; eugenics; environmental protection; rejection of the modern art movement and an embrace of classical art; and defense of the Nazi flag.

Police State

A police state is a form of a **totalitarian political system**. A nation does not identify itself as a police state; rather, the characterization is applied by critics of the nation. A **police state** is regulated by police, who exercise power on behalf of an executive authority. It is very difficult to challenge the police and question their conduct in a police state, and there is no rule of law; the law is simply the will of the leader. The police state is based on the concept of enlightened despotism, under which the leader exercises absolute power with the goal of providing for the good of a nation; opposition to government policy is an offense against authority and, therefore, against the nation itself.

Because public dissent is not allowed, people who oppose the government must do so in secret. Therefore, the police must resort to the use of informers and secret police to seek out dissenters.

Westminster System

The Westminster system is a form of **representative democracy**, modeled after the system used in the United Kingdom's Palace of Westminster, where the UK Parliament is located. Features of the **Westminster system** include an executive branch comprised of members of the legislature; a Cabinet made up of senior members of the executive branch; the existence of opposition parties; an elected legislature or a system comprised of two houses, one of which is elected and the other of which is appointed; and a ceremonial head of state, who is distinct from the head of government, and who may hold reserve powers that are not usually exercised. Members of parliament are elected by popular vote, and the head of government is selected via an invitation from the head of state to establish an administration. The head of government, referred to as the **prime minister**, must control a majority of seats within the lower house of parliament or must ensure that there is no absolute majority against them.

Domestic Policy and Foreign Policy

Domestic policy entails all government policy decisions, laws, programs, plans, actions, and behaviors that address **internal state matters**. Examples of **domestic policy** include tax policy, social security and welfare programs, environmental laws and regulations, and regulations on businesses and their practices. In contrast, **foreign policy** addresses how a country will **engage with other countries**. Foreign policy is typically created to protect and promote a country's national interests, national security, ideological goals, and economic prosperity. Foreign policy can be directed toward peaceful cooperation with other countries, as well as towards aggression, war, or exploitation. The creation of foreign policy is typically the responsibility of a country's head of government and foreign minister. In the US, the legislature also has substantial power and influence, which is reflected in the authority of Congress to pass **Foreign Relations Authorization bills**.

World Government and Comparative Politics

Study of Comparative Politics

In a **unitary government**, power is centralized. There are subdivisions or departments of the unitary government that are responsible for carrying out laws, but these bodies do not draft or pass legislation. Small countries with an ethnically and culturally homogenous population are more likely to have a unitary government. A **federal government**, on the other hand, is broken down into subdivisions, usually called states or provinces. These subdivisions are given some legal jurisdiction, though the central government usually has final authority. A large country with a diverse population is likely to have a federal government. Finally, a **confederation** is a collection of states that, while all sending representatives to a central government, do not grant the central government much power. Confederations are prone to disintegration.

Ways in Which Governments May Be Organized

Comparativists, or those who study **comparative politics**, place the political events of the present in a **historical context**. In general, these academics are concerned with creating overarching political theories that can be applied to all sorts of situations. To this end, they focus on governmental structure and its effects on the behavior of a nation and its citizenry. Comparative political scientists are especially concerned with the development and evolution of nations over time.

Parliamentary vs. Proportional Representation Forms of Government

The officials in a parliamentary government are not elected; instead, they are **selected** by their party. Candidates for **parliament** are put forth by various political parties and elected by the people. The leader of the majority party in a parliamentary system is called the **prime minister**. The prime minister takes other members of parliament to serve as his or her **cabinet**, or advisory council. One interesting feature of the parliamentary system is that elections are not held at regular intervals but are instead called by the prime minister at his or her discretion. On the other hand, in a **proportional representation** system, the electorate casts ballots for a particular **party** rather than for an **individual candidate**. Each party is given a number of seats in the legislature proportionate to its share of the vote. When there is no dominant or majority party, disparate parties must join together to create a coalition government.

Normative vs. Empirical Questions Asked by Comparativists

Comparativists must grapple with normative questions, which deal with the ethical value of political actions, and empirical questions, which concern matters of fact. In some sense, a **normative question** can only be answered with an opinion. For this reason, many political scientists eschew this sort of question. For example, comparative political scientists may avoid questions related to the morality of certain systems of government or certain political actions. Comparative political scientists are more likely to attend to **empirical questions**, which can be settled through investigation. For instance, a political scientist might try to determine the effects of different geographies or political structures on the development of a nation because many aspects of these topics can be explored through research and statistical analysis.

States, Nations, Regimes, Governments, Politics, and Political Science

- **State**: any country that has an established border, a fixed population, and its own organized government
- **Nation**: a state whose citizens share a language, a culture, and—often—a religion
- **Regime**: a particular iteration of government in a nation, usually headed by a charismatic leader. For example, Iraqis suffered for many years during the Saddam Hussein regime.
- **Government**: an organized institution responsible for making and enforcing laws in a particular area and for a particular people
- **Politics**: the set of behaviors and activities that relate to the operation of government
- **Political science**: the academic discipline concerned with the structure and operation of government

Purpose and Organization of Government

Originally, governments were created to **protect citizens and their property**. Although government systems have evolved a great deal since these origins, the basic intent is the same. There are governments representing all types of human groups. Even the smallest tribe has some sort of **organization and leadership structure**. In most cases, a national government is predicated upon a populace with a shared language and culture as well as a large and powerful middle class. This is not always the case, however, as evidenced by Canada, which has English and French Canadian as its official languages. There are several different organizational structures for governments, including communism, socialism, theocracy, confederation, hereditary monarchy, constitutional monarchy, democracy, and tribal council.

Comparative Politics

Differences in Scope and Method of Study

Comparativist political scientists are usually affiliated with one of three main approaches: rational choice comparativism, structuralism, or culturalism. A **rational choice comparativist** uses mathematics and statistics to explore politics and government. The work of a rational choice comparativist is similar to that of an economist. A **structuralist**, on the other hand, looks for similarities in political behavior in different contexts, with the aim of constructing broad, overarching theories. A structuralist seeks to advance theories that can be applied to many different nations. Finally, a **culturalist** emphasizes the details on the ground. These academics visit and often live among the people they are studying. They amass a great deal of data, which they are often reticent to apply outside of the specific context in which it was obtained.

Cultural Approach to Research

Culturalists pay particular attention to the political and cultural orientation of villages and small groups. They view **culture** as a lens through which to view **politics**. The only theories produced by culturalists are those having to do with the particular group being studied. During the 1980s and '90s, academia moved away from the culturalist approach, favoring instead the pseudo-mathematical precision of the structuralists. Another reason for the decline of the culturalist approach is the expense associated with long research trips; governments and universities have become less willing to fund these sorts of ventures.

Structural and Rational Choice Approaches to Research

As much as possible, structuralists try to rely on data gathered in the field; however, some of this data can be difficult to trust. **Rational choice political scientists**, on the other hand, rely almost exclusively on mathematics, statistics, and game theory. These academics are also interested in universally applicable theories, but they rely solely on **data** and exclude anecdotal information.

Theory of Decisions

In comparative government, the **theory of decisions** is the idea that personal political choices are influenced both by the beliefs and experiences of the decision maker and by the information provided to him. To some extent, the actors in a political system are dependent on the quality of information they receive. However, the members of a polity are likely to make vastly different decisions based on the same information. Comparative political scientists try to isolate those personal and environmental factors that exercise significant influence on political decisions.

Inference

An inference is a conclusion based on an established set of information. While an **inference** is not itself a fact, it should be based on facts. A **deductive inference** proceeds from general statements to a specific conclusion. The following is a classic example of deductive reasoning: "All men are mortal. Socrates is a man. Therefore, Socrates is mortal." **Inductive reasoning**, by contrast, proceeds from specific examples to general ideas. The following is an example of inductive reasoning: "Socrates is a man. Socrates is mortal. Therefore, all men are mortal." In political science, and especially in comparative political research, inferences are needed to make conclusions about political behavior. Some comparative political scientists focus on granular, on-the-ground research, which they use to create general theories. Other comparativists create general theories in the opposite direction by moving from general principles to specific applications.

Ideas of Dependency Theory

According to dependency theory, financial and natural resources naturally shift from **poorly developed countries** to **industrialized countries**. In other words, this theory asserts that rich states will tend to become richer, and poor states will tend to become poorer. Before this theory was advanced, many political scientists had believed that all states have a tendency toward industrialization and that the differences between states are simply due to varying degrees of progress along this path. However, dependency theory suggests that underdeveloped countries may never become developed if they are not given special assistance. Indeed, those who support this theory assert that today's underdeveloped countries are relatively less developed than any of today's industrialized countries ever were. Wealthy countries exploit the cheap labor and resources of underdeveloped nations, thereby perpetuating underdevelopment.

Policy Challenges Faced by Governments

Governments strive to meet the needs and desires of the people, but they are often restrained by **cost**. Of course, there are often disagreements between rival factions over the proper course of legislation. To pay for necessary services, a government may need to raise **taxes**, which will not be appreciated by the public. In the modern world, governments are mainly preoccupied with issues like the environment, health care, infrastructure, the economy, education, and foreign relations.

Constitution of the Federal Republic of Nigeria

In 1999, the Nigerian government affirmed a new constitution without submitting it for public approval. The **Nigerian constitution** is largely based on that of the United States: It divides the government into **legislative, judicial, and executive branches**, and it establishes **two legislative houses**. It also enumerates the fundamental **rights of Nigerians**. The Nigerian constitution asserts that political parties must be national and must have their headquarters in the capital city of Abuja. To win the presidency, a candidate must receive a majority of the total votes and at least one-quarter of the votes in two-thirds of the states. The point of these restrictions is to avoid domination by one ethnic group, though one of the practical results is to encourage two-party politics. An odd omission in the constitution was highlighted in 2009, when President Alhaji Umaru Yar'Adua fell ill. The constitution had no protocol for succession, so Vice President Goodluck

Jonathan did not have any authority when he took over. The legislature had to be assembled in a hurry to issue a special act allowing Jonathan to govern.

Constitution of Mexico

When devising their constitution, Mexico's legislators were concerned about the possibility of a single ruler dominating the country for decades. For this reason, they forbade the president from serving more than one six-year term. Also, Mexican politicians are forbidden from seeking reelection to the same office. Despite these provisions in the constitution, Mexico was dominated by the **PRI party** for years. Mexican presidents exploited the system for their own gain. The **Mexican constitution**, which was drafted on February 5, 1917, arranges the government in much the same way as that of the United States. **Article 123** outlines workers' rights including the eight-hour workday, the right to strike, and a mandatory day of rest. Until this provision was ratified, Mexico had been the scene of rampant worker exploitation. As of 2005, capital punishment was outlawed in Mexico.

Constitution of the Post-Communist Russian Federation

In 1993, Boris Yeltsin led the effort to draft and pass a constitution of the **Russian Federation**. This constitution established a government with a **strong executive branch,** somewhat limited by a legislature and a judiciary, as well as a system of checks and balances. However, whenever a national emergency was claimed, the president was allowed to seize control, dissolving the legislature and, if he desired, initiating national referenda or elections. It quickly became clear that even though this government was ostensibly ruled by the legislature, the executive could maneuver his way to a preeminent position rather easily.

Great Britain's Lack of a Written Constitution

Great Britain is an interesting model of a nation that remains stable despite **not having a formal constitution**. Britain does depend on King John's **Magna Carta of 1215** and the **Act of Settlement of 1701** (which describes the line of royal succession), but national affairs are governed in large part by case law and historical precedent. If a majority of both houses of Parliament approve, the "constitution" can be amended. This process is only complete, however, when the queen gives her royal assent. In general, the British system is founded on the supremacy of Parliament and the rule of law. In other words, **Parliament** is affirmed as the primary legislative body in the nation with the authority to determine the royal succession, control royal authority, and mandate term limits for its members.

Types of Regimes

- **Regime**: a type of government, or the duration of a particular government or leader's control in a country.
- **Authoritarian regime**: organizational structure in which one person or a small group controls the political, educational, financial, economic, and diplomatic functions of the country.
- **Totalitarian regime**: a regime that is organized around a central idea. Perhaps the best example of a totalitarian regime is the National Socialist state that existed in Germany between 1936 and 1945. Adolf Hitler and the other leaders of this movement promoted the idea that Germans were a master race engaged in a battle to the death with other ethnic groups. In the Soviet Union, leaders like Lenin and Stalin based a totalitarian regime around the idea of class struggle. In a totalitarian regime, government control is pervasive, and it is difficult for citizens to obtain or disseminate information contrary to the interests of the regime.

- **Democratic regime**: a system in which citizens have the ability to vote directly on the issues or to elect leaders. Some of the varieties of democracy include presidential, parliamentary, and veto player.

Authoritarian Regime of Joseph Stalin in the Soviet Union

Vladimir Ilyich Lenin founded the communist **Soviet Union** and was succeeded by **Joseph Stalin**. Stalin's **totalitarian** regime aimed to industrialize the country, in part by forcing the migration of peasants to the cities. Stalin stopped at nothing in pursuit of his plan. He murdered thousands of farmers who resisted forced migration, and his program for turning over the countryside to collectives resulted in massive famines that killed millions. Stalin's so-called "Five-Year Plans" established unrealistic goals for industrial production and then imposed harsh living conditions on citizens in pursuit of these goals. Stalin died in 1953, with the blood of perhaps 20 million people on his hands. Stalin's successor, Nikita Khrushchev, repudiated him in 1956.

Regime of Mikhail Gorbachev in Russia

In 1985, Mikhail Gorbachev became general secretary of the Communist Party in the Soviet Union. **Gorbachev** had three goals: **perestroika**, or industrial reform; **democratization**; and **glasnost**, or openness to the rest of the world. None of these initiatives was wholly successful. His campaign for industrial reform was stymied by production managers who did not want to take responsibility. Meanwhile, his democratization efforts resulted in the election of candidates who were not members of the Communist Party. For instance, Boris Yeltsin, not a member of the Communist Party, was elected president in 1991. Finally, the glasnost policy foundered because members of the news media were not allowed to criticize current leaders or policies, though they were permitted to criticize the leaders and policies of the past. Ultimately, Gorbachev was forced to resign, and on December 25, 1991, after surviving an attempted coup, he broke up the Union of Soviet Socialist Republics (USSR).

Regime of Boris Yeltsin in Russia

After the resignation of Gorbachev and the disbanding of the USSR, **Boris Yeltsin** took over as president of the Russian Federation. The **constitution** he delivered in 1993 placed a great deal of power with the executive, but it was approved by Russian voters. Some members of the **Duma** from the communist era conspired to overthrow Yeltsin, but he put down this nascent rebellion. Rather than gradually introduce a market economy, Yeltsin attempted "shock therapy," which caused **hyperinflation** at rates higher than 100 percent. Meanwhile, Moscow and St. Petersburg were overtaken by criminal gangs. In 1995, Russians elected very conservative and communist candidates, and in 1996, Yeltsin won reelection only because he was supported by a coalition of wealthy businessmen. His second term was marked by illness and miscalculations, leading to the crash of the ruble in 1998 and Yeltsin's ultimate **resignation** on December 31, 1999.

Regime of Vladimir Putin in Russia

Yeltsin was replaced by his final prime minister, a former KGB official named **Vladimir Putin**. Putin would prove to be a strong leader, evidenced early on by his military invasion of Chechnya after a separatist group from that region was blamed for the bombing of a Moscow apartment building in 1999. This invasion played well with the Russian populace, and after the **Unity Party**, which backed Putin, dominated the elections of December 1999, Putin himself was elected president the following March. He was able to improve the Russian economy, but the **Chechen War** dragged on, and crime became a major problem in the cities. In the 2003 elections, control of the Duma was seized by the **United Russia party**, which supported Putin. At this point, Putin's rule became more autocratic; he took control of the media and intimidated many would-be challengers to his presidency. He won reelection in a rout in 2004. The Russian constitution forbade Putin from running again in 2008, but his handpicked successor, **Dmitry Medvedev**, won the election and immediately installed Putin as prime minister, where he continues to exercise a major influence.

Totalitarian Regime of Mao Zedong in the People's Republic of China

In 1949, Mao Zedong began his twenty-seven-year reign as self-styled paramount leader. His major goal was to **industrialize** China, which at that time was a largely agrarian society. The **Great Leap Forward,** initiated in 1958, was an ambitious fifteen-year plan for modernization. It was a disaster, marked by crop shortages and starvation, and it was ultimately discontinued after only two years. Another communist program, the **Cultural Revolution**, lasted from 1966 to 1976. This was an attempt to ingrain communist values and eliminate any subversion. Youths, known as the **Red Guard**, were encouraged to turn in those they suspected of disloyalty. Those unlucky enough to be detained for subversion were beaten, sent to work camps for "reorientation," and often killed. At the same time, the Red Guard was tasked with destroying all the artifacts of pre-communist China, including buildings, artworks, and historic texts.

Authoritarian Regime of Deng Xiaoping in China

In 1976, Mao Zedong died, creating a power vacuum. After a struggle, **Deng Xiaoping** wrested control from Mao's widow, leader of the so-called "Gang of Four." After assuming the mantle of paramount leader, Deng initiated a program that loosely translates as "socialism with Chinese characteristics." This program focused on four areas of **modernization**: business, farming, education, and the military. Deng created special economic zones for foreign investment in large Chinese cities. At the same time, Deng's "mass line" approach motivated peasants to sell their surplus crops, and citizens were forbidden from having more than one child. One of the final events of the Deng period was the massacre of unarmed pro-democracy protesters in **Tiananmen Square** in 1989.

Authoritarian Regime of Jiang Zemin in China

The programs of the Deng regime were, for the most part, continued by **Jiang Zemin**. The government was very concerned with preventing any future episodes like Tiananmen, so the Chinese justice system became even more oppressive. Moreover, Jiang continued the **internal passport system**, which prevented Chinese citizens from moving freely throughout the country. The **Falun Gong**, a group of religious dissidents, was harshly repressed, and **Tibet** was prevented from asserting independence. However, Jiang also promoted the **Special Economic Zone program** and worked to get China admitted to the **World Trade Organization**. He also enabled the campaign that brought the 2008 Summer Olympics to Beijing. Both Macao and Hong Kong rejoined China but were allowed to maintain their local governments, an arrangement known as "one country, two systems." Taiwan declined to enter China this way. In 2002, Jiang Zemin retired at the age of 76.

Structure and Party Makeup of Legislature of Great Britain

Although Great Britain is nominally ruled by a **monarch**, the real power resides with **Parliament**. Great Britain does not have a written constitution; instead, it relies on historical precedent and case law. The country's legislature consists of a **House of Lords** and a **House of Commons**. Membership in the House of Lords is hereditary. This house can create bills, but it does not have very much power. The House of Lords serves as the highest court of appeals in Great Britain. The members of the House of Commons, on the other hand, are elected. This body is run by a **prime minister**, selected by the representatives of the majority party. In recent years, the **New Labour Party** and the **Conservative Party** have dominated British politics, though the **Liberal Democrats** have been gaining prominence. The leadership of the majority party has the responsibility for calling elections, though they must do so within five years of taking office.

Controversial Regime of Conservative Party Margaret Thatcher

When Margaret Thatcher became prime minister of Great Britain in 1979, she vowed to wrest control of the country from the **union leaders** who had gained so much power under Labour Party governments. She also strove to create a more muscular foreign policy, resulting in the **Falklands Crisis** with Argentina in 1982. In 1984 and 1985, Thatcher suppressed striking coal miners, making good on her pledge to marginalize unions. At the same time, she turned several government-owned industries over to private concerns. Some of these businesses included British Steel, Rolls Royce, and British Petroleum. Thatcher discontinued the practice of subsidizing housing, and she sold all houses owned by the state. During her regime, taxes and inflation declined, but unemployment and homelessness grew. She became increasingly controversial, and in 1990, John Major was selected as prime minister by the Conservative Party.

Regime of Conservative Party Prime Minister John Major

John Major was relatively inexperienced when he became prime minister, a situation that was not helped by the almost immediate controversy over Britain's entry into the **European Union**. British people were especially opposed to the idea of adopting the euro and abandoning the pound. Major handled that issue by putting it to a public vote, but his administration continued to be bedeviled by minor scandals and crises like mad cow disease. Though it was perhaps not his fault, Major seems to have presided over the end of a Conservative era in British politics. He resigned in 1995, and the **New Labour Party** took control of Parliament in 1997.

Regime of New Labour Party Prime Minister Tony Blair

In 1997, the New Labour Party took control of Parliament and installed **Tony Blair** as prime minister. Although his party was considered leftist, Blair was more moderate and indeed moved to have **socialism** removed from the New Labour Party's charter. Blair placed a premium on **public opinion** and called for referenda on all sorts of controversial issues, as for instance the relative independence of Northern Ireland, Wales, and Scotland. Blair also queried the British public on EU membership, adoption of the euro, and peace with Northern Ireland. During the Blair administration, Britain adopted a minimum wage law and further diminished the voting rights of the House of Lords. Although the New Labour Party retained control in 2007, Gordon Brown succeeded Blair as prime minister.

Single-Party Authoritarian Regime of the PRI in Mexico

Even though its 1917 constitution made room for multiple political parties in the federal system, Mexican politics was dominated by the **Institutional Revolutionary Party (PRI)** for 70 years. Furthermore, Mexican presidents wielded exceptional power. Although PRI candidates were in control from 1929 to 2000, they changed their positions quite a bit over time. Indeed, the policy swings of the PRI were part of a "**pendulum theory**" designed to maintain control of the government. Each PRI president would handpick his successor, a process known as ***el dedazo***. Of course, the PRI's control was aided by its domination of the news media, which allowed the party to control the information available to voters and repress any attempt at subversion.

Regime of Mexican President Carlos Salinas

Carlos Salinas became president of Mexico under a cloud of suspicion: The computer tallying election results had crashed right after displaying a slim lead for Democratic Party of the Revolution (PRD) candidate Cuauhtémoc Cárdenas. After it had been repaired, the computer showed Salinas in the lead. Despite this dubious beginning, Salinas quickly earned domestic and international support by privatizing highway construction, airlines, mines, banks, and the telephone service, and by joining the United States and Canada in the **North American Free Trade**

Agreement (NAFTA). Unfortunately, any economic progress was undone by a currency crash in 1993, and Salinas's popularity was further diminished by ongoing bloody conflict in Chiapas with a rebel peasant group known as the Zapatistas. Salinas had planned for Luis Donaldo Colosio to succeed him, but Colosio was assassinated in Tijuana in 1994. The blame for this murder and the killing of PRI's secretary general in Mexico City was pinned on Raúl Salinas, the president's brother, who also was caught with a considerable amount of stolen money. Carlos Salinas was so unpopular at the end of his term as president that he had to flee to Ireland.

Regime of Mexican President Ernesto Zedillo

Ernesto Zedillo became known as the "accidental president" of Mexico because he only became the PRI candidate after the murder of Luis Donaldo Colosio. As president, Zedillo borrowed extensively from the United States to shore up the Mexican economy. At the same time, he **modernized PRI** by empowering the *técnicos* (technocrats) and diminishing the power of *los dinos*, the party's old guard. Zedillo also improved the election process by allowing observers, installing computer vote counters, creating voter cards, and establishing an independent election authority known as IFE. Moreover, he broke the tradition of handpicking his successor, instead creating a **primary system** for PRI candidates. Although Zedillo can be praised for these actions, the short-term result was that PRI lost some of its stature in Mexico.

Regime of Mexican President Vicente Fox

With the election of **PAN** party candidate **Vicente Fox** in 2000, Mexico had a president who was not a member of PRI for the first time since 1917. Fox had a background in business, as president of Coca-Cola's Mexican operation, and in government, as governor of the state of Guanajuato. He immediately tried to negotiate a better immigration policy with the United States, but these efforts were unfortunately derailed by the terrorist attacks of September 11, 2001. In the wake of 9/11, the United States was unwilling to cooperate on a deal that would admit more foreigners. At the same time, Fox struggled to reach legislative compromises with the PRI and PRD representatives, and he continued to be weighed down by the ongoing conflict in Chiapas. Though Fox was able to make some positive changes to the Mexican judiciary, his declining popularity was demonstrated by the primary defeat of his handpicked successor, Santiago Creel. In the end, though, Fox was succeeded by Felipe Calderón, another member of the PAN party.

Ibrahim Babangida's Military Regime in Nigeria

Nigeria has endured a series of oppressive military regimes, not the least of which was led by **Ibrahim Babangida**. In 1985, Babangida took control of Nigeria and pledged to restore civilian rule after he had fixed the workings of the government. To do so, however, he claimed that it was necessary to move the capital to an ethnically mixed location, mandate a two-party-only system, take a new census, forbid current and former politicians from seeking office again, and create ethnically mixed states by redrawing boundaries. In a hopeful sign, Babangida called for local elections in 1992. However, when Moshood Abiola appeared to win the election, Babangida invalidated the results, claiming fraud. Violent riots ensued. The popular perception of Babangida was not improved by subsequent revelations that he had amassed an enormous fortune while in office.

Sani Abacha's Military Regime in Nigeria

Babangida's rule was tranquil compared to that of his successor, **Sani Abacha**. Abacha took over control of Nigeria in 1993 and immediately began a campaign of violence against his political adversaries. Abacha's victims included **Moshood Abiola**, who most analysts believe defeated Babangida in the 1992 election, and Abiola's wife. Former leader **Olusegun Obasanjo** was jailed on trumped-up charges, and Nobel Prize-winning author **Wole Soyinka** was forced into exile. Indeed, the Abacha regime drove much of Nigeria's intelligentsia out, which had calamitous economic consequences. A particularly low moment was the execution of ten **Ogonis**, including the writer Ken Saro-Wiwa, who were protesting the destruction of farmland by oil companies, most notably Shell. Abacha's death in 1998 led to the creation of a new constitution known as the **Fourth Republic**. The freed Obasanjo took control of the Nigerian government in 1999 amid great hope, but he was unable to quell the tribal conflict.

Islamic Regime in Present-Day Iran

In the present organization of **Iran**, the most powerful person is the religious leader known as the **faqīh**. The faqīh, at present **Ali Hosseini-Khamenei**, has power over the military, the judiciary, and the media. Iran is a self-styled Islamic Republic with a **unicameral legislature**, whose 209 members serve four-year terms. Iran does not allow political parties, and most political power in Iran is vested in the **Council of Guardians** (which selects the candidates for parliament) and the Supreme Court. From 2005 to 2013, the president of Iran was **Mahmoud Ahmadinejad**. During his term, the nation moved forward on a nuclear program while attempting to diversify its oil-based economy. International observers considered Ahmadinejad's 2009 reelection to be highly dubious. Ahmadinejad was succeeded by **Hassan Rouhani** in 2013, and he remains the current president after being reelected in 2017. Ahmadinejad tried to run for a third term in both 2013 and 2017, but his nomination was rejected by the Council of Guardians both times.

Socialism, Communism, Capitalism, and Mixed Economies

In a socialist system, both the means of production and the land are owned by the state, which means that the wealth generated by economic activity is also distributed by the state. Nevertheless, a **socialist state** may have regular elections and a functional legislative body. The following northern European countries are considered socialist: Romania, Poland, Hungary, Bulgaria, Sweden, Ukraine, Belarus, Russia, and Armenia. The **communist system** is similar insofar as the means of production and the land are owned by the state, but it is typical for political life to be dominated by one party, often in a totalitarian manner. North Korea, Vietnam, Cuba, and China are all communist countries, though China has successfully introduced some elements of capitalism. The **capitalist system** places control of the means of production and the land in the hands of private interests. Finally, in a **mixed economy**, control over the economy is divided between private citizens and the government. In other words, the government controls some functions and leaves others to citizens.

How Fascist Governments Achieved Legitimacy During the 1930s and 1940s

Even the most immoral governments can be **legitimate** as long as they are stable and respected by their own citizens and the governments of other countries. For instance, during the 1930s and 1940s, the **Nazis** in Germany and the **fascists** in Italy achieved legitimacy because they were highly stable and conducted diplomacy with other governments. This legitimacy was achieved despite rampant abuse of human rights by both of these regimes. Similarly, **China** and **Iran** are currently considered legitimate, even though they are notorious violators of human rights and even though Iran is seeking to obtain nuclear weapons against the protests of the rest of the international community.

Communism as the Guiding Principle of the People's Republic of China

In the People's Republic of China, the government is run by a single party, the **Communist Party**. For much of China's history, communist principles like government ownership of the land and the means of production were sacrosanct. However, some of these restrictions have been eased in recent years, and China has become more capitalist. Nevertheless, even though China allows private ownership and supports foreign investors, it remains avowedly communist. For example, the

Chinese government has suppressed all criticism of the communist system, most infamously in the Tiananmen Square massacre of 1989. Suppression of public discourse continues, and in 2000, Google declined to offer some of its services to China amid complaints that the government was using the internet to crack down on dissidents. In 2018, China removed the two-term limit of the presidency that had been established in the 1990s, effectively allowing the current president **Xi Jinping** to remain in office for life. His political philosphies have been amended into the country's constitution known as "Xi Jinping thought."

Socialist States vs. Communist States

In the socialist and communist systems, the government owns the vast majority of the means of production. Indeed, in **communist countries**, the government owns all industry. In China, for instance, the government owns the land, though it is willing to lease out some parcels to private farmers. In a communist state, dissent is not tolerated, and the government strictly controls the information available to citizens. **Socialist states**, on the other hand, do not place all industries under government control. Generally, socialist governments control public services like telephone companies, healthcare providers, and transportation businesses, while leaving other industries to be run by private owners. To fund the essential services under government control, the public is typically charged very high taxes in a socialist system.

Mexico's Decentralized Government

In Mexico, a great deal of political power is vested in the state governments. Each state has a governor, a state legislature, and a state police force. Mexicans vote for local offices and elect people to represent their region in the two legislative bodies of the central Mexican government: the **Senate** and the **Chamber of Deputies**. Although the structure of the Mexican government is decentralized, the domination of the **PRI party** concentrated an inordinate amount of power in the central government for much of the country's history. In 2000, with the victory of Vicente Fox, a member of the heretofore marginal **PAN party**, PRI's rule came to an end.

Centralized Government of Iran

The government of Iran is highly centralized, with most of the power vested in the Islamic leader known as the **faqīh**. The central government creates and passes legislation, and the local governments are tasked with enforcing this legislation. The **Majlis** (legislative body) consists of 290 members who are unaffiliated with any political party, as political parties are illegal in Iran. A set of twelve **mullahs**, appointed by the faqīh and known as the **Council of Guardians**, delimits the authority of the Majlis. For instance, only candidates approved by the Council of Guardians may attempt to enter the Majlis, and the Council of Guardians retains the right to veto any legislation it dislikes.

International Factors Influencing a Country's Public Policy

Public policy can also be influenced by **international factors**. For instance, **economic treaties** will adjust the incentives for various public policy actions. They will also determine the extent to which a country regulates its imports, exports, and tariffs. Many nations have **military treaties** as well. For instance, the United States has declared that it will support Taiwan should the island nation be invaded by China. In some countries, political instability leads to inaction. One example would be Nigeria before 1999; uncertainty about the military government made it difficult for the nation to engage in international trade. Some nations, like Iran, become pariahs internationally and have a hard time cooperating on trade agreements for that reason. Finally, many nations decide public policy issues based on their perceived effects on the value of that nation's own **currency** relative to the currencies of other nations.

Chapter Quiz

Ready to see how well you retained what you just read? Scan the QR code to go directly to the chapter quiz interface for this study guide. If you're using a computer, simply visit the online resources page at **mometrix.com/resources719/clepamergov** and click the Chapter Quizzes link.

Constitutional Underpinnings of American Democracy

United States Constitution

Presidential Succession Act of 1947

The Presidential Succession Act of 1947 established that if both the President and the Vice President are unable to execute the powers and perform the duties of the Presidency, the position will be assumed by the **Speaker of the House**, followed by the **President pro tempore of the Senate**, and then the **Cabinet members** in the following order: Secretary of State, Secretary of the Treasury, Secretary of Defense, Attorney General, Secretary of the Interior, Secretary of Agriculture, Secretary of Commerce, Secretary of Labor, Secretary of Health and Human Services, Secretary of Housing and Urban Development, Secretary of Transportation, Secretary of Energy, Secretary of Education, Secretary of Veterans Affairs, and Secretary of Homeland Security.

Marbury v. Madison

Marbury v. Madison was an 1803 Supreme Court case that established a standard for the constitutional power of the Supreme Court to carry out **judicial review of Federal statutes**. The Supreme Court decided that it had the power to invalidate a statute that it found to be in violation of the Constitution. The case set the judicial branch as an equal counterpart to the other two branches of the United States federal government. Specifically, Marbury v. Madison was the inaugural case during which the United States Supreme Court used the power of judicial review.

Review Video: Marbury v. Madison
Visit mometrix.com/academy and enter code: 573964

Judicial Review

Courts possess the power of **judicial review**, which entails reviewing laws or official actions made on the part of government representatives to determine if those laws or actions are in violation of the Constitution. In the United States, the power of judicial review is held by courts. Specifically, the **United States Supreme Court** holds the highest power to make decisions regarding the constitutionality of both state and federal laws. The doctrine of judicial review was founded based on the decision of the Supreme Court in the case of Marbury v. Madison in 1803. In states, the power of judicial review lies with the highest appellate court, which can be referred to as a **Supreme Court** or the **Court of Appeals**.

Bill of Rights

Creation of the Bill of Rights

The Bill of Rights includes the first ten amendments to the Constitution. These amendments were proposed to the states by the first Congress of the United States of America as a means to protect personal and civil liberties. The **Bill of Rights** was originally composed of twelve amendments, which were proposed by Congress on September 25, 1789. In 1791, the group of ten amendments that comprise what is known as the Bill of Rights was ratified by the states. These amendments became part of the Constitution of the United States.

Amendments 1-5

The **First Amendment** protects the five most important civil liberties of citizens of the United States. These civil liberties include the freedom of religion, the freedom of speech, the freedom of the press, the right of assembly, and the freedom to petition. The **Second Amendment** protects the right to bear arms. The **Third Amendment** protects the right of citizens not to have troops placed in their private homes. The **Fourth Amendment** protects citizens against search and seizure of their private homes without a warrant. The **Fifth Amendment** pertains to the rights of an accused person and protects the right to a trial, the right not to be tried twice for the same crime (double jeopardy), and the right against self-incrimination. The Fifth Amendment also protects the right of citizens against the taking of their private property without just compensation.

Amendments 6-10

The **Sixth Amendment**, like the Fifth Amendment, pertains to the rights of an accused person and protects the right to a speedy trial. The **Seventh Amendment** protects the right to a jury trial in civil cases. The **Eighth Amendment** places limitations on bail fines and protects against cruel and unusual punishment. The **Ninth Amendment** protects the rights of citizens that are not specifically identified in the Constitution and states that such rights shall be respected by the federal government. The **Tenth Amendment** states that certain powers are retained by the states and by the people.

Reconstruction Amendments

The Thirteenth, Fourteenth, and Fifteenth Amendments are known as the **Reconstruction Amendments**. They are grouped in this manner because they were passed during the Reconstruction period following the Civil War. They were drafted with the purpose of abolishing slavery, preventing slavery under other names, and extending rights to all citizens of the United States, regardless of race or color. Specifically, the **Thirteenth Amendment**, which was ratified in 1865, abolished slavery in the United States. The **Fourteenth Amendment**, which was ratified in 1868, established limitations on states such that no state may deny any citizen equal protection under the laws. The **Fifteenth Amendment**, which was ratified in 1870, established the right of citizens to vote regardless of race or color.

Nineteenth Amendment

The Nineteenth Amendment gave **women the right to vote**. This amendment was proposed on June 4, 1919, and was ratified on August 18, 1920. An amendment to give women the right to vote was first introduced in Congress in 1878, but it failed to pass. For the next four decades, the amendment was reintroduced in every session of Congress but was defeated each time. The involvement of women in the war effort during World War I spawned increased support for women's suffrage. Finally, in 1918, the House of Representatives approved the amendment to grant women suffrage, but the Senate defeated it. In 1919, the Senate also passed the amendment and sent it to the states for approval, where it was ratified in 1920.

Twenty-fifth Amendment

If the Presidency is vacated, the **Vice President** becomes President. If the Vice Presidency is vacated, the President **nominates** a Vice President, who must be approved by a majority vote in Congress. If the President informs Congress that he is unable to execute the powers and duties of the Presidency, the Vice President assumes the Presidency until the President informs Congress that he is able to return to office. Similarly, the Vice President will assume the Presidency if the Vice President and a majority of the Cabinet inform Congress that the President is unable to serve as President, and the President may resume office if he informs Congress that he is able to do so. The

Vice President and the Cabinet can counter the President's assertion that he is able to resume office, and by a two-thirds vote within Congress, the Vice President will continue to act as President.

Review Video: Bill of Rights
Visit mometrix.com/academy and enter code: 585149

Articles of Confederation

The very first constitution in the history of the United States was the **Articles of Confederation**. The Articles of Confederation served as a plan for the government of the United States and was created on the principles that were defended during the Revolutionary War. However, the Articles of Confederation contained weaknesses. Specifically, the Articles of Confederation did not assign the power to create and collect taxes, did not assign power to oversee trade, and created a relatively weak executive power without the ability to enforce legislation. The greatest fault of the Articles of Confederation was that it did not originate with the people, but rather power was vested in the **states** to avoid a central government authority. Under the Articles of Confederation, every state could collect its own taxes, issue currency, and maintain its own militia, creating inefficiencies in the national government. The national government was primarily responsible for foreign policy and treaties. The Articles of Confederation provides learning opportunities and was a stepping stone in creating the Constitution.

Review Video: Articles of Confederation
Visit mometrix.com/academy and enter code: 927401

Governing Principles of the Constitution

The governing principles of the United States Constitution include the principle of **popular sovereignty**, which is associated with a system of government that is created by the people, for the people. Other governing principles of the United States Constitution include the rule of law, the Supreme Court, judicial review, the separation of powers, and the system of checks and balances. In addition, the governing principle of **federalism** guided the formulation of the United States Constitution, allowing for the sharing of power between the federal government and the states. The governing principles of the Constitution also included individual rights, which are embodied in the **Bill of Rights**.

Documents that Influenced the Writing of the Constitution

There are a number of documents that influenced the writing of the United States Constitution. The **Mayflower Compact** was influential; it was written in 1620 by the first settlers in the New England colony. The **Virginia Declaration of Rights** was written in 1776 and served as a prototype for other state constitutions and for the Bill of Rights. The **Declaration of Independence** was also adopted in 1776 and was influential in the writing of the Constitution. The **Articles of Confederation** was adopted in 1781 and served as the first constitution for the original thirteen states following the American Revolution. The **Federalist Papers** also served as an influence for the drafters of the US Constitution; they were published in newspapers to encourage ratification of the Constitution, which was ratified in 1788.

Review Video: Drafting the Constitution
Visit mometrix.com/academy and enter code: 662451

International Influences on the Development of the US Constitution

The US Constitution was written with the influence of **international sources and factors**. While a number of the concepts represented in the US Constitution were unique, others were taken from classical political theories and from the British model of mixed government. Specifically, the US Constitution was influenced by sections of the **Magna Carta**, which was written in the year 1215. Another influential document in the drafting of the US Constitution included the **English Bill of Rights**, which was established in 1689. Specifically, as in the English Bill of Rights, the US Constitution mandates a trial by jury, includes the right to bear arms, and bans the application of extreme bail amounts and cruel and unusual punishments.

US Constitution

The US Constitution represents the highest law within the United States. It was the successor of the Articles of Confederation and was finished in 1787, adopted by the Constitutional Convention in Philadelphia, and subsequently ratified by the thirteen original states. The **US Constitution** established a federal union of sovereign states as well as a federal government to oversee the union. The US Constitution went into effect in 1789 and has been a model for constitutions created within other nations. The Fourteenth Amendment of the Constitution provides all United States citizens with **equal protection** under the Constitution. The judiciary branch of the federal government has the power to review the constitutionality of laws passed in the United States and can strike down laws if they are determined to be **unconstitutional**. The Fifth Article of the Constitution addresses how Congress may propose Constitutional **amendments**. In addition, a convention consisting of at least two-thirds of the states can propose Constitutional amendments. Amendments must be ratified before they become part of the Constitution.

Process of Making Amendments to the US Constitution

The process for making amendments to the US Constitution is outlined in **Article Five** of the Constitution. **Amendments** can be proposed by either two-thirds of both chambers of the United States Congress or by a convention of at least two-thirds of the legislatures of the states. Before an amendment can be included in the Constitution, it must be **ratified** by three-fourths of the legislatures of the states, or by three-fourths of special conventions that have been assembled in each of the states for the purpose of ratifying the Constitutional amendment. The President of the United States plays no official part in the process of making constitutional amendments. To date, twenty-seven amendments have been ratified and included in the Constitution.

Constitutional Interpretation

Originalism

The term *originalism* encompasses a set of theories regarding **constitutional interpretation**. People who are proponents of **originalism** believe that the meaning of the Constitution does not evolve, but is fixed and should be followed and upheld by Judges. Originalism as a form of constitutional interpretation is often favored by individuals who associate themselves with conservative political ideals in the United States. There are numerous theories that fall under the category of originalism. These theories include **original intent**, which is the opinion that Constitutional interpretation should agree with the originally intended meaning of the people who wrote and ratified the Constitution. A second theory is **original understanding**, which represents the view that people interpreting the Constitution should seek evidence of what the people who drafted the Constitution understood the Constitution to mean. The third and most followed originalist theory is **original meaning**, which is the opinion that interpretation of the Constitution should be founded on what the meaning of the words would have been at the time the Constitution was ratified.

Strict Constructionism

Strict constructionism is a form of judicial interpretation restricting judicial interpretation to the **literal meaning** of the words and phrases found in laws. **Strict constructionism** does not allow for other sources to be used or for assumptions to be made about the meaning of the laws beyond the literal words and phrases. Individuals who are proponents of strict constructionism only read text that is explicitly pertinent, and do not permit legislative intent or metaphysical ideas to influence their interpretation. People who support strict constructionism believe that if a legislative body desires to enact a law, its members are knowledgeable about how to draft it and pass it in the words that express their exact intent and meaning and that, therefore, the judiciary should not be responsible for reconstructing what the intent of the legislative body was.

Judicial Activism

Judicial activism is a form of constitutional interpretation in which judicial decisions do not adhere to **precedent** or extend beyond the **limits of conventional law**. In reality, any ruling which does not fall within the limits of conventional expectations could be construed as an example of **judicial activism**. Judges are sometimes accused of judicial activism regardless of their political affiliations and views and regardless of their philosophies regarding judicial interpretation. Critics of judicial activism are concerned that judges who make decisions based on their personal beliefs are not interpreting laws on sound principles. In the US, the accusation of judicial activism often carries a negative connotation and refers to decisions that are made to further the interests of specific social or political goals. Specific acts that are associated with judicial activism in the US include the declaration that a law is unconstitutional when it is not; supporting a law that is unconstitutional; overturning judicial precedent; and ruling against the words or intent of laws or the Constitution.

Living Constitution

The term *Living Constitution* is often used to describe the capacity of Congress or of the states to make **amendments** to the United States Constitution. Specifically, it refers to the process of how amendments can be made that is stated in Article Five of the Constitution. The term *Living Constitution* is also often applied to characterize how the interpretation of a number of sections within the Constitution has evolved with the application of the Constitution to real-world cases throughout the history of the United States since the Constitution was adopted.

Textualism

The theory of textualism is a form of **constitutional and statutory interpretation**. Specifically, proponents of **textualism** argue that the literal meaning of the Constitution or of a statute should guide the interpretation of the Constitution or of the statute. Individuals who support textualism do not believe that non-textual resources should be used to interpret the Constitution or statutes, such as the legislative intent that was meant when the law was passed, the issue that the law was meant to address or fix, or the important questions of the judge and impartiality of the law.

Prudentialism

There exist three prudential standing principles, which means that they were judicially created. Congress can override **prudential standing principles** by passing a statute. The three prudential standing principles are Prohibition of Third-Party Standing, Prohibition of Generalized Grievances, and the Zone of Interest Test. **Prohibition of Third-Party Standing** requires that individuals can only declare their own rights and cannot declare the rights of a third party not before a court. **Prohibition of Generalized Grievances** requires that a plaintiff cannot sue if an injury is broadly shared in a similar way with a large number of individuals. The **Zone of Interest Test** is divided into two tests that are applied by the US Supreme Court. The first is the Zone of Injury, in which the nature of the injury is such that Congress expected would be covered by the statute. The second is the Zone of Interests, in which the individual is within the zone of interest covered by the statute or by the Constitution.

Constitutional Standing Requirements

The three constitutional standing requirements are injury, causation, and redressability. A plaintiff in a case must have suffered an **injury**, which is defined as an offense against a legally protected interest. An injury is required to be actual, imminent, distinct, and palpable, not abstract. There must also exist a **causal** connection between the injury and the action that the plaintiff is complaining about. Finally, it has to be highly probable and not simply speculative that a decision in favor of the plaintiff will **redress** the injury caused to the plaintiff. Congress does not have the power to alter the three **constitutional standing requirements**.

State, County, and City Government

City Government

Approximately eighty percent of the United States population resides in **urban areas** or areas immediately surrounding urban areas. Therefore, **city governments** are an integral part of the general system of government within the United States. City governments provide direct services to their citizens, even more so than the federal government or state governments. Examples of services that are provided by city governments include police forces and firefighting forces, health and sanitation, education, public transportation, and housing. City governments are chartered by state governments; the city charter outlines the objectives and powers allocated to the city. While many city governments operate independently from state governments, many large cities work in collaboration with state and federal governments. The organization of city governments varies, but the majority have a **central council** that is chosen by the people through an election, as well as an **executive officer** who is aided by department heads. Traditionally, there are mayor-council city governments, commission city governments, and city manager city governments.

County Government

A county is a subregion within a state. Counties typically consist of at least two towns and a number of villages. Usually, a single city or town within a county is named as the **county seat**. The county seat serves as the site at which government offices are situated. The county seat is also where the board of commissioners for the county convenes. Small counties have boards that are selected by the entire county. In contrast, large counties have commissioners who represent each town, city, or district within the county. **County boards** are responsible for setting county taxes, appropriating funds, setting pay rates for county personnel, overseeing county elections, building and upkeep of highways and bridges, and managing federal, state, and county social welfare programs.

Town and Village Government

Many governments are too tiny to be classified as city governments. Such small jurisdictions are known as **towns** and **villages** and receive a charter from a state. Town and village governments address only **local matters** such as maintaining local roads, illuminating local roads, managing a local water supply, maintaining local police and firefighting forces, developing and implementing local health policies, providing or organizing the disposal of waste locally, setting local taxes, and managing local schools. Town and village governments are typically overseen by a board or a council that is chosen through election. A chairperson or a president can serve as the chief executive officer of the board or council. Alternatively, an elected mayor can serve as the chief executive officer of the board or council. Town and village governments can be staffed by clerks, treasurers, police and fire officers, and health and welfare officers.

Town Meetings

Some local governments hold what are referred to as **town meetings**. Town meetings have occurred for more than two hundred years. The townships that hold town meetings are typically found throughout New England states. Town meetings are a rather unique characteristic that distinguishes some small-town governments from other forms of government. Town meetings are typically held on an annual basis, but they can be held more often if necessary. At a town meeting, registered voters assemble in an open meeting to elect officers, discuss local matters, and vote on local legislation that concerns the operation of the local government. The attendees of the town meeting make decisions together as a community concerning issues such as road maintenance, building public facilities, tax rates, and town budgets.

State versus Federal Government

Initially, government systems in the United States were characterized as **state governments** that were essentially self-governed. These circumstances in the early days of the United States represented an aversion to the **centralized government** that was present in England, the colonial power that first controlled America. The state government system proved to be insufficient, and, therefore, the **Constitution** was written to delineate the powers afforded to a **federal government**. The Constitution also delineates the relationship between the federal and state governments. The system instituted in the Constitution is known as a federalist system, in which powers are shared between the federal and state governments. Specific powers are allocated to the federal government, while other powers remain in the hands of state governments.

Concurrent Powers

While both the national and state governments reserve specific powers that the other does not have, there are certain powers that are shared between them. These shared powers are known as **concurrent powers**. The concurrent powers that are shared by both the national government and the state governments include the power to collect taxes, the power to build roads, the power to borrow money, the power to create courts, the power to create and enforce laws, the power to establish banks and corporations, the power to spend funds in the interest of the general welfare of the United States and its citizens, and the power to take private property for purposes that benefit the public so long as just compensation is provided.

State Constitutions

In the United States, state governments each have a unique **state constitution**. State constitutions resemble the federal Constitution in many ways. However, state constitutions may not be in disaccord with the federal Constitution. State governments have control over affairs that occur **within state boundaries**, such as communications within state boundaries; regulations concerning property, industry, business, and public utilities; criminal codes; and labor conditions. There are also numerous matters over which state and federal governments **share jurisdiction**. State constitutions differ from one another regarding some issues, but they are typically laid out similarly to the federal Constitution. All state constitutions contain a section on people's rights and a section that outlines how government should be organized. Every state constitution also stipulates that ultimate authority rests with the people and establishes specific standards and values as the basis of government.

State Executive and Legislative Branches

State governments are divided into executive, legislative, and judicial branches, just as in the federal government. In a state government, the **governor** serves as the head of the **executive branch**. The governor is elected by popular vote for a term of either two or four years, depending on the state. Every state in the US has a **bicameral legislature** except Nebraska, which has a single legislative body. The bicameral legislature is divided into an upper house and a lower house. The upper house is typically referred to as the **Senate**, as in the federal government, and the lower house can be referred to by a number of names, including the **House of Representatives**, the **House of Delegates**, or the **General Assembly**. State senators typically serve for a term of four years, while members of the House of Representatives, House of Delegates, or the General Assembly serve for a term of two years.

State and Local Courts

Every state has a **court system** that is independent and distinct from the federal court system. The hierarchy of the state court system includes **trial courts** at the lowest level; **appellate courts** are the highest courts in the state court system. The great majority, over ninety-five percent, of the court cases in the United States are heard and decided in state courts and local courts, which also fall under the jurisdiction of the states. Depending on the state, there may be one or two appellate courts within the state. States organize and name their courts differently. Typically, lower courts are assigned specific names and authority to hear specific types of cases, such as family courts and probate courts. Beneath the specialized trial courts are more informal trial courts, including magistrate courts and justice of the peace courts, which typically do not involve a jury.

Mayor-Council City Governments

The mayor-council form of city government has existed the longest among the types of city governments in the United States. In a city where there is a **mayor-council** form of government, there is a **mayor** who is elected by the people to serve as the chief executive officer of the city. There is also a **city council** that is elected by the people. The members of the city council represent the regions that make up the legislative branch. The mayor is responsible for appointing the people who head the numerous city departments. The mayor can also appoint other city officials. The mayor has the power to veto the laws of the city, which are also referred to as city ordinances. The mayor may also draft the budget for the city. The city council is responsible for passing the laws of the city, establishing city property taxes, and allocating funds among city departments.

Commission City Governments

The commission form of city government represents a blending of the executive and legislative duties into one assembly of city officials known as the **city commission**. There are typically three or more members of the city commission, and they are chosen in a city-wide election. Every member of the city commission is charged with overseeing the responsibilities of at least one department of the city. One member of the city commission is selected to be the chairperson of the commission. The chairperson of the city commission is sometimes referred to as the mayor of the city. However, the chairperson of the city commission does not have any power above and beyond that of the other members of the city commission.

City Manager City Governments

The city manager form of city government began in an effort to meet the needs of complicated issues that are common in modern-day American cities. Meeting this complicated mix of issues requires experience and knowledge in a variety of matters, as well as managerial skills. Traditional elected officials do not always hold such skills, knowledge, and expertise. To overcome this problem, some city governments have opted to have a single individual serve in the position of **city manager**, with the responsibility for exercising executive powers. City governments based on the city manager system have a relatively small **city council** that is chosen through election. This city council creates city ordinances and develops city policies. The city manager is hired by the city council to implement the laws and policies developed by the council. The city manager is also responsible for creating a city budget and overseeing city departments. There is typically no limit to the amount of time that an individual may serve in the position of city manager.

Separation of Powers in State and Local Governments

Government at both the federal and state levels is characterized by a **separation of powers**. At the local level, the organization of government is different. State and local government often distinguishes between **executive powers** and **law enforcement powers** by allowing citizens to choose public prosecutors through elections. In some states citizens elect judges as well. In local governments, the election of individuals who represent special authority, such as police chiefs and members of school boards, serves to separate such individuals from the executive and legislative branches of government. At the local level, juries also have a significant role in maintaining the system of checks and balances, as they have the sole authority to determine the facts in most criminal and civil cases, restricting the power of the executive and judicial branches in enforcement of laws.

Powers of State Governments

Each state government reserves the **power** to issue state licenses, the power to regulate business and commerce within the boundaries of the state, the power to hold elections, the power to create local governments, the power to ratify Constitutional amendments, and the power to regulate public health and safety. The state governments may also exercise powers that are not explicitly stipulated in the United States Constitution as being held by the federal government. Similarly, the state governments may exercise powers that the Constitution does not explicitly restrict the states from exercising.

Powers of the Federal Government

The national, or federal, government reserves **powers that are not afforded to the states**. The national government has the power to print money, regulate business and commerce between states and between the United States and other countries create treaties and carry out foreign policies, declare war, maintain military forces, and create post offices. The national government also has the power to create laws that are deemed essential to carrying out all of the other powers that are constitutionally granted to the national government.

Powers Denied to State Governments

There are a number of powers that are denied to state governments within the United States of America. These **restrictions** are stipulated by the **Constitution** of the United States. States are restricted from doing anything that the federal government is restricted from doing. States are also restricted from forming alliances or confederations. States are restricted from declaring war and maintaining navies. State governments are restricted from making and entering into treaties with foreign countries. In addition, state governments are restricted from making money. State governments are also restricted from placing taxes on imports and exports from or to other states, respectively. States are restricted from preventing the requirements of a contract from being met as well. Finally, states are restricted from taking away an individual's rights without due process of law.

Powers Denied to the Federal Government

There are a number of powers that are denied to the national, or federal, government of the United States of America. These **restrictions** are stipulated by the **Constitution** of the United States. The federal government is restricted from breaking or abusing the Bill of Rights. The federal government is also restricted from placing taxes on exports from one state to another state. In addition, the federal government is restricted from using funds from the United States Treasury unless an appropriations bill is passed and approved. Finally, the federal government is restricted from altering state borders.

Powers Denied to Both the Federal Government and State Governments

There are a number of powers that are denied to both the federal government and state governments in the United States of America. These **restrictions** are stipulated by the **Constitution** of the United States. The federal government and state governments are restricted from conferring titles of nobility. Both levels of government are also restricted from allowing slavery to take place; this restriction is specifically stated in the thirteenth amendment of the United States Constitution. The federal and state governments are also restricted from prohibiting citizens of the United States from exercising their right to vote based on race, color, or based on previous conditions of servitude; this restriction is specifically stated in the fifteenth amendment of the United States Constitution. Finally, both the federal and state governments are also restricted from prohibiting citizens of the United States from exercising their right to vote based on gender; this restriction is explicitly stated in the nineteenth amendment of the United States Constitution.

Appeals

If a case originates in a state court, it typically must be **appealed** within the state court system and have exhausted all possible appeal options within the state court system before it is possible to appeal the case within the federal court system. Also, in order for a case that has originated within the state court system to be appealed within the federal court system, the case must have something to do with a **federal issue**. If a decision is made by a state supreme court and the case involves a federal issue, it can be appealed to the US Supreme Court. The US Supreme Court then has the authority to overturn state laws.

Police Powers of the State Courts

State courts have the authority to exercise what are referred to as **police powers** over specific issues. These issues include health, morals, and safety. For example, in order to ensure the health of citizens, a state government can mandate that all children enrolled in school must receive vaccinations against particular diseases. If anyone wanted to challenge such a mandate issued under the police power of the state, they would have to do so in a state court. Police powers are granted by the **tenth amendment** of the United States Constitution. However, most state constitutions also include a Bill of Rights unique from the federal Bill of Rights that restricts the state's power over its citizens.

State Court Judges

State court judges may take their seats in state courts in a number of ways. State judges can be **appointed** to state courts by a state governor. After a specific period of time has elapsed, these appointed judges may run in an election. State judges can also be initially **elected** to their seat in a state court, rather than first being appointed. Elections for judgeships are sometimes contested and partisan in nature. However, sometimes elections for these positions are not contested and not partisan in nature. States often try to better state and local judges by establishing pools of qualified legal professionals for state governors to select appointees from.

State Legislatures

There are over seven thousand state legislators throughout the fifty states. Term limits exist for these legislatures in a number of states, but not all. There are also over thirty-five thousand staff members that have positions with state legislatures.

ORGANIZATION AND PROCEDURES OF STATE LEGISLATURES

The organization and procedures of state legislatures serve as the foundation for state legislatures. Specifically, the key procedural components of state legislatures include **parliamentary procedures**; every state legislature establishes its own parliamentary procedures. Procedures also include those that are in place to effectively and efficiently operate **committees**; most legislatures have created personnel policies to organize the staff that carries out everything from research to security and from budgeting to technology support. State legislatures are organized at many levels in order to ensure that legislative staff members are working effectively and efficiently. One of the means of ensuring organization is through legislative sessions and session dates. **Legislative sessions** can be characterized as regular legislative sessions, which meet at regularly scheduled intervals, or as special or extraordinary legislative sessions, which are called by either the governor of a state or by the legislature itself with the purpose of addressing specific issues.

TIED CHAMBERS IN STATE LEGISLATURES

A tied chamber occurs in a state legislature when the political parties represented in the legislature are equally divided. Usually, this is not the case. Normally, one political party has control over the state legislature. However, in recent times it has become more common for state legislative chambers to be **divided equally** along party lines. Such an equal division along party lines does not necessarily mean that there will be a political deadlock within the state legislature. There are a number of methods that state legislatures use to move forward past a stalemate, including a coin toss, a vote by the lieutenant governor, statutory laws to guide legislatures through a deadlock situation, and negotiated agreements.

Chapter Quiz

Ready to see how well you retained what you just read? Scan the QR code to go directly to the chapter quiz interface for this study guide. If you're using a computer, simply visit the online resources page at **mometrix.com/resources719/clepamergov** and click the Chapter Quizzes link.

CLEP Practice Test

Want to take this practice test in an online interactive format?
Check out the online resources page, which includes interactive practice questions and much more: **mometrix.com/resources719/clepamergov**

1. Congress possesses all of the following enumerated powers EXCEPT the power to

a. regulate commerce.
b. appoint federal judges.
c. establish post offices.
d. declare war.

2. Why can the House of Representatives often agree on new legislation faster than the Senate?

a. The Senate is more partisan than the House of Representatives.
b. The Senate's Debate Committee often makes agreement difficult.
c. The House has stricter limits than the Senate for debate time.
d. The House does not require proposed bills to go to committee first.

3. A filibuster can be used to

a. kill proposed legislation in the Senate by extending debate indefinitely.
b. kill proposed legislation in the House by extending debate indefinitely.
c. prevent a bill from leaving a committee by extending debate indefinitely.
d. override a veto on a new bill by extending debate indefinitely.

4. Which of the following is the BEST description of the trustee view of representation?

a. Representatives are entrusted to vote in accordance with the views of their constituents and therefore should do so.
b. Representatives should vote their consciences and in order to serve the nation as a whole.
c. Representatives are entrusted to bring tangible benefits to their constituents and should work to do so.
d. Representatives should vote in accordance with the principles of the political party to which they belong.

5. The majority party in Congress has the authority to do all of the following EXCEPT

a. choose the Speaker of the House and the Senate majority leader.
b. hold the majority of congressional committee seats.
c. require congresspersons to vote with the party line.
d. choose the chairpersons of all congressional committees.

6. Which of the following is a way in which Congress does NOT exercise its oversight function?

a. Holding hearings
b. Conducting investigations
c. Changing an executive agency's budget
d. Firing executive branch officials

7. The purpose of a conference committee is to reach an agreement

a. between the House and the Senate.
b. between the executive branch and Congress.
c. between the entire Senate and a committee.
d. between standing committees and party leadership.

8. Logrolling is the practice of

a. attaching riders to a new bill.
b. trading votes between legislators.
c. strategically scheduling votes.
d. benefiting wealthy interest groups.

9. What is the purpose of proposing a new bill under a closed rule?

a. To limit the number of speakers on the floor during debate
b. To prevent amendments from being added to new legislation
c. To impose strict time limits on debate on the floor
d. To overrule a committee's recommendation about new legislation

10. Why is it easier to add amendments to bills in the Senate than in the House of Representatives?

a. Party leadership in the Senate has more formal power than party leadership in the House of Representatives.
b. Because Representatives often represent more local interests than Senators, the House of Representatives is typically less partisan then the Senate.
c. The Speaker of the House, unlike the Senate majority leader, is free to add amendments to a bill.
d. Riders can be added to bills in the Senate, but not to bills in the House of Representatives.

11. Which of the following activities does the House Rules Committee control?

a. Scheduling what bills to debate and when they are debated
b. Selecting who will speak during floor debate
c. Appointing members for standing committees
d. Selecting the Speaker of the House

12. A power that the House of Representatives has that the Senate does NOT is the power to

a. try impeached government officials.
b. approve proposed treaties.
c. introduce bills about revenue.
d. confirm presidential appointments.

13. A power that the Senate possesses that the House of Representatives does NOT is the power to

a. impeach government officials.
b. approve proposed treaties.
c. declare war on another nation.
d. provide oversight of the executive branch.

14. How does the president exercise a pocket veto?

a. By accepting some lines in a bill and rejecting others
b. By attaching a signing statement to a bill
c. By failing to sign a bill when Congress has finished its term
d. By refusing to read the text of a proposed bill

15. Which BEST describes the relation between the president and the Congress regarding legislation?

a. The president generally leads Congress regarding national policy issues.
b. Congress drafts legislation within the limits of the president's proposed budget.
c. Key congressional committees report to the president about new bills.
d. Presidential officials serve as honorary advisers on congressional committees.

16. Executive privilege is the power of

a. the executive branch to carry out laws.
b. the president to appoint officials to federal posts.
c. executive officials to keep information from Congress.
d. the president to lead the U.S. armed forces.

17. In what way can the president act as a legislator?

a. By serving as head of state
b. By serving as commander-in-chief
c. By appointing diplomats
d. By issuing executive orders

18. The president has the authority to do all of the following EXCEPT

a. recognize foreign governments.
b. keep troops in military action for an indefinite amount of time.
c. negotiate treaties with other nations.
d. command the military to use nuclear weapons.

19. The president's official cabinet typically includes which of the following officials?

a. National Security Council and White House Office officials
b. The Senate majority leader, Chief Justice, and Secretary of State
c. Leaders of the fifteen executive departments
d. Un-appointed friends and advisers to the president

20. Which of the following is the BEST description of a signing statement?

a. A statement a president makes upon signing legislation into law
b. A statement of a president detailing his/her reasons for a veto
c. A statement a president makes expressing disappointment in a failed bill
d. A statement of a president's desires for new legislation

21. The president CANNOT issue a pardon in the case of

a. persons related to the president.
b. officials who serve the president.
c. persons convicted of treason.
d. impeached government officials.

22. When can the vice president vote in the Senate?

a. Always
b. Never
c. When a vote is tied
d. When a senator is absent

23. What does the term capture refer to in regards to federal regulatory agencies?

a. The loss of efficiency due to increasing bureaucratic rules and red tape
b. The tendency of agencies to serve the interests of the industries they regulate
c. The president's ability to appoint individuals to lead regulatory agencies
d. The difficulty of effectively overseeing very large regulatory agencies

24. What is the BEST description of the power or powers of regulatory agencies?

a. Executive power only
b. Executive and legislative powers
c. Executive, legislative, and judicial powers
d. Executive and judicial powers

25. One way government corporations differ from private corporations is that government corporations

a. are barred from earning profits.
b. lack a board of directors.
c. receive no federal funding.
d. lack any stockholders.

26. The merit system in government includes the practice of

a. hiring on the basis of exam results.
b. hiring on the basis of campaign work.
c. rewarding departments for swift action.
d. rewarding departments for wise spending.

27. Which of the following is one way Congress might limit the power of the bureaucracy?

a. Dismiss civil servants
b. Use the Office of Management and Budget
c. Enact a sunset law
d. Use the National Security Council

28. Which is the BEST description of whistle blowing?

a. Conducting a congressional investigation
b. Prosecuting governmental wrongdoing
c. Reporting bureaucratic mismanagement
d. Stopping funding for inefficient programs

29. Which is the BEST description of the relationship between the bureaucracy and the three branches of the national government?

a. The bureaucracy implements presidential policy only.
b. The bureaucracy implements legislative policy only.
c. The bureaucracy implements presidential and judicial policy.
d. The bureaucracy implements policies/rulings of all three branches.

30. An independent executive agency

a. is a member of the Cabinet.
b. reports directly to the president.
c. is run by a board of directors.
d. receives no congressional funding.

31. What are the three components of an iron triangle?

a. Legislators, interest groups, and bureaucrats
b. Congress, the judiciary, and the president
c. Bureaucrats, interest groups, and the media
d. Legislators, the media, and the president

32. What is agenda setting in relation to the media?

a. Influencing what issues the public believes are important
b. Framing the news to promote a certain political viewpoint
c. Serving as a watchdog over the national government
d. Offering media access to government officials

33. Which of the following statements is FALSE?

a. Televised debates help shape the public's perceptions of presidential candidates.
b. Perceptions of media bias are often due to a viewer's own political views.
c. Interest groups prefer the internet over television.
d. The government can prevent publication of some sensitive information.

34. What does enabling legislation do?

a. Give additional authority to an administrative agency
b. Streamline an administrative agency
c. Require increased oversight of an administrative agency
d. Create an administrative agency

35. The process of incorporation of the Bill of Rights regards

a. amending state constitutions to include a Bill of Rights.
b. ratifying the Bill of Rights in the U.S. Constitution.
c. applying rights in the Bill of Rights to state government action.
d. gaining widespread political and popular support for the Bill of Rights.

36. How does the power of judicial review limit the power of one branch of the federal government?

a. It enables the Supreme Court to judge the constitutionality of actions taken by the president.
b. It allows Congress to review and vote on the President's nominations to federal courts.
c. It gives the president the authority to reject court rulings that violate established federal law.
d. It permits the Supreme Court to impeach the President for violating state or federal laws.

37. Which of the following rights are guaranteed by the First Amendment of the Constitution?

a. Freedom of speech, freedom of religion, freedom from self-incrimination
b. Freedom of speech, due process, freedom from search and seizure
c. Freedom of speech, freedom of assembly, due process
d. Freedom of speech, freedom of religion, freedom of assembly

38. The establishment clause means that the federal government is forbidden to

a. try a person more than once for the same crime.
b. establish a state-sponsored religion or promote one religion over another.
c. censor newspaper materials that the government finds objectionable.
d. disband existing federal courts except in case of emergency.

39. How did the Supreme Court case of Engel v. Vitale bear on the freedom of religion in the United States?

a. The Court ruled that state-sponsored school prayer violated the Constitution.
b. The Court ruled that any prayer in public schools violates the Constitution.
c. The Court ruled that states cannot pay for students to attend religious schools.
d. The Court ruled that religious groups cannot meet on public school property.

40. In Griswold v. Connecticut, the Supreme Court ruled that citizens have a right to privacy on the grounds that

a. the Fourth Amendment lists such a right.
b. it was established by Roe v. Wade.
c. it is implied by other rights specified in the Bill of Rights.
d. Congress has legislated such a right.

41. Which of the following is the BEST description of prior restraint?

a. The power of the executive branch to censor to preserve national security
b. The assumption that defendants are proven innocent until guilty
c. The legal inability to imprison citizens prior to probable cause
d. The legal inability of the government to forbid free expression before the fact

42. According to the clear and present danger test, speech can be restricted when

a. the government follows due process.
b. speech presents a clear and present danger.
c. a speaker has citizenship in a foreign nation.
d. speech is slanderous or libelous.

43. The equal protection clause of the Fourteenth Amendment requires

a. state governments to apply the law equally.
b. the federal government to apply the law equally.
c. private companies and organizations to provide equal access.
d. private companies and organizations to provide equal services.

44. The Supreme Court has original jurisdiction over cases that involve

a. domestic citizens being accused of treasonous activities.
b. domestic citizens' violations of the federal tax code.
c. opposing state governments or violations of the federal tax code.
d. opposing state governments or foreign diplomats.

45. Which is the BEST description of how the Supreme Court decides which cases to review?

a. The Court accepts cases of important legal significance and broad consequences.
b. The Court chooses cases that involve a potentially unconstitutional use of power.
c. The Court accepts as many cases as possible, within the limits of a reasonable workload for each justice.
d. The Court chooses cases that at least four justices believe were mistakenly decided by a lower court.

46. Which is the BEST description of stare decisis?

a. The legal requirement of the executive branch to obey established law
b. The legal requirement of state courts to be guided by Supreme Court rulings
c. The principle that judicial rulings should follow established precedent
d. The principle that judicial rulings should follow the Constitution

47. The U.S. district courts hear cases that involve

a. federal civil law only.
b. both federal criminal and civil law.
c. state criminal law only.
d. both state criminal and civil law.

48. Which of the following BEST describes the relationship between the federal appeals courts and the Supreme Court?

a. Appeals court judges compile a list of potential cases for Supreme Court review.
b. Appeals courts review cases after they have been rejected by the Supreme Court.
c. A Supreme Court justice monitors each circuit of appeals courts.
d. Supreme Court justices must first serve as appeals courts' judges.

49. Judicial restraint is the view that the judiciary should

a. interpret the Constitution according to the likely intentions of its authors.
b. use the power of judicial review to restrain unconstitutional government actions.
c. adhere to the strict wording of laws and defer to legislatures.
d. follow the principles and wishes of the executive branch of government.

50. By what process do U.S. appeals courts typically make their decisions?

a. A jury makes decisions about the facts of a case.
b. A jury reviews a case based on lower court records.
c. A panel of judges makes decisions about the facts of a case.
d. A panel of judges reviews a case based on lower court records.

51. The due process clause of the Fourteenth Amendment forbids

a. the federal government from depriving citizens of life, liberty, or property without following proper legal procedures.
b. the federal government from depriving citizens of freedom of speech, religion, and assembly without following proper legal procedures.
c. state governments from depriving citizens of life, liberty, or property without following proper legal procedures.
d. state governments from depriving citizens of freedom of speech, religion, and assembly without following proper legal procedures.

52. What is the tradition of senatorial courtesy?

a. Requiring a ¾ majority vote in the Senate to confirm appointments to appeals courts
b. Seeking the advice of the Senate Judiciary Committee about nominations to the Supreme Court
c. Allowing senators to formally appoint judges to federal district courts
d. Consulting a state senator or senators about nominations to federal district courts in the senator's (or senators') state

53. A main difference between a political party and an interest group is that

a. interest groups have little influence on legislation.
b. political parties seek formal control of government operations.
c. interest groups are free to use the media to promote candidates.
d. political parties want to advance an agenda.

54. Which of the following was a main component of the Democratic Party (associated with Andrew Jackson) in the 1820s?

a. A focus on wealthy Americans
b. Federal spending on infrastructure
c. Expanded government programs
d. Racism toward African Americans

55. What BEST explains the rise of the Democratic Party over the Republican Party during the 1930s?

a. The Democratic Party opposed additional civil rights for minorities.
b. The Republican Party favored Prohibition, which was unpopular.
c. President Hoover was ineffective in addressing Great Depression suffering.
d. Voter turnout was low as people struggled with other issues.

56. Which is the BEST description of a primary purpose of political parties?

a. Enunciating political policies
b. Establishing ties with interest groups
c. Raising funds for political purposes
d. Attracting widespread support

57. Which of the following typically happens at the national convention of a political party?

a. Selection of candidates for state offices
b. Formulation of the party's platform
c. Election of the national chairperson
d. Voting to select key candidates' positions

58. Which of the following statements about interest groups is true?

a. Citizens' groups are contrasted with ideological groups.
b. There are more citizens' groups than other interest groups.
c. Economic groups typically promote a public good to gain members.
d. Economic groups enjoy many competitive advantages over citizens' groups.

59. Which of the following illustrates the concept of a free rider?

a. Enjoying tax-funded roads without paying taxes
b. Passing legislation to support an interest group
c. Attaching an unrelated amendment to a bill
d. Electing a candidate with interest group funds

60. Which of the following is NOT an example of direct lobbying?

a. Providing information to legislators
b. Holding mass demonstrations
c. Helping draft legislation
d. Testifying before Congress

61. Why would an interest group use outside lobbying in addition to inside lobbying?

a. To demonstrate popular support for the group's position
b. To avoid media attention during scandals
c. To withdraw interest group donations
d. To establish closer relationships with legislators

62. How much money can an interest group's political action committee (PAC) donate to an individual political candidate for federal office?

a. $5,000
b. $10,000
c. As much as the PAC wants
d. No money at all

63. Which of the following statements is true?

a. PAC donations to campaigns play little role in those campaigns.
b. There are just a few interest groups with significant influence.
c. Most members of Congress do not receive PAC money.
d. The influence of interest groups is biased toward the wealthy.

64. Which of the following BEST describes the relationship between PACs and incumbents?

a. PACs tend to donate to incumbents.
b. PACs tend to want incumbents to be defeated.
c. Incumbents cannot receive PAC donations.
d. Incumbents typically don't need PAC donations.

65. According to the pluralist argument in favor of interest groups participating in politics,

a. interest groups effectively represent diverse interests in society.
b. the small number of interest groups prevents them from becoming too powerful.
c. interest groups have more influence than ordinary citizens.
d. the number of interest groups makes government more cost-effective.

66. A blanket primary is a primary in which voters

a. can vote for party candidates even if the voters do not belong to that party.
b. can vote only for candidates who belong to the voter's registered party.
c. rank order their top three candidates.
d. choose between minority party candidates.

67. In a state with a Republican governor and Republican control of both state legislative bodies, the state party organization must be run by

a. the governor.
b. the Speaker of the House.
c. the senate majority leader.
d. whoever is appointed chairperson.

68. Voters with low incomes tend to vote

a. more liberally on social issues.
b. more with the center on social issues.
c. more liberally on economic issues.
d. more with the center on economic issues.

69. Voters who frequently attend church are more likely than others to vote

a. Republican.
b. Democrat.
c. Libertarian.
d. as independents.

70. What is the BEST definition of the term sampling error regarding a public opinion poll?

a. A problem with the size of the poll sample
b. A problem in the selection of the people polled
c. An assessment of how accurate the poll is
d. An assessment of the wording of the poll

71. Typically, how important is a person's family upbringing regarding how a person feels about politics?

a. Slightly important
b. Very important
c. Not at all important
d. Moderately important

72. What is the BEST definition of civil disobedience?

a. Demonstrating in favor of civil liberties legislation
b. Demonstrating in favor of civil rights legislation
c. Disobeying any law in a peaceful, nonviolent manner
d. Conscious disobedience of a law thought to be unjust

73. In which of the following regions would you most likely encounter "red" (Republican) states?

a. West Coast
b. Northeast
c. Rocky Mountains
d. Northern Midwest

74. The "lifestyle effect" is a correlation between political views and which of the following?

a. Economic status
b. Age
c. Region
d. Education

75. How important is the media in how Americans learn about politics?

a. Not at all important
b. Slightly important
c. Moderately important
d. Very important

76. Why might public polls fail to gauge public opinion accurately?

a. Polling is inherently inaccurate.
b. A sample might represent an entire population.
c. People might invent an opinion if they don't have one.
d. A sample might be random.

77. The public's trust in the government can be said to

a. be consistently high.
b. be consistently low.
c. fluctuate .
d. hover in the middle.

78. How is an exit poll conducted?

a. By asking people about the effectiveness of specific officials
b. By a random telephone survey on election days
c. By asking people to evaluate an administration at the end of its term
d. By polling voters as they leave voting sites

79. Which of the following statements about public opinion is true?

a. It can significantly affect the power of the president.
b. It has no effect on what the government does.
c. It typically offers precise recommendations for government action.
d. It is ignored by the government except during election years.

80. Women are more likely than men to oppose

a. rights for lesbians and gays.
b. the use of military force.
c. spending on social programs.
d. affirmative action programs.

81. The majority of Americans

a. are very informed about political affairs.
b. often shift their allegiance between parties.
c. identify themselves as liberals.
d. do not have a consistent ideology.

82. What is the main idea of the majoritarianism theory of democracy?

a. Government policy should follow the wishes of the majority.
b. The public good is best served by governments that are democratic.
c. The majority can implement policy best through direct democracy.
d. Government should do whatever will help the most people.

83. How did Shays' Rebellion influence the formulation of the Constitution?

a. It promoted the creation of a Bill of Rights.
b. It illustrated the need for a stronger central government.
c. It showed the weakness of the federal army.
d. It demonstrated Congress's inability to regulate commerce.

84. Which of the following was NOT a motivation for the Great Compromise in the formulation of the Constitution?

a. To protect the power of small states
b. To provide a check on the power of the general public
c. To convince small states to agree to the Constitution
d. To protect Northern states' ability to limit slavery

85. Which of the following BEST describes the federal government's structure of separation of powers?

a. The three branches of government have strictly separate powers.
b. The three branches of government have separate but overlapping powers.
c. Legislative power is divided between the House and the Senate.
d. Legislative power is divided between the legislative and executive branches.

86. James Madison advocated a system of checks and balances because

a. he had read John Locke's theory of checks and balances.
b. he believed that, without one, factions could destroy the government.
c. he wanted to ensure a weak national government.
d. he had read Jean-Jacques Rousseau's theory of the social contract.

87. Which of the following is the BEST description of the origin of U.S. federalism?

a. It was a synthesis of John Locke's political theories and the ideas of Baron de Montesquieu.
b. It was modified from the model of an existing government to limit national power.
c. Americans invented it as a compromise to disagreements about the scope of state versus national authority.
d. It was adopted to limit the power of the general public over the federal government.

88. Which of the following is a concurrent power?

a. Police power
b. Foreign policy power
c. Power to regulate commerce between states
d. Power to regulate commerce strictly within states

89. According to the elastic clause of the Constitution,

a. the national government has the power to formulate the supreme law of the land.
b. the national government has powers that are implied by the Tenth Amendment.
c. the national government's powers vary according to different circumstances.
d. the national government has powers necessary for exercising its enumerated powers.

90. Which of the following is an example of cooperative federalism?

a. State laws which are more progressive than national government laws
b. Joint emergency response by state and government officials
c. Agreements between states on commercial issues
d. Separation of tax powers between states and the national government

91. Minority rights in traditional democratic theory refers to the principle that

a. a one-person/one vote system typically protects the rights of the minority.
b. democracy typically infringes on the rights of the minority.
c. the majority should not legally infringe on the rights of the minority.
d. there is no sharp distinction between majority and minority rights.

92. According to the pluralist theory of democracy,

a. democracy produces a very diverse society.
b. interest groups usually negatively affect the public good.
c. legislation is often passed through compromise.
d. government is run by a small group of minority groups.

93. Which of the following features of the national government BEST illustrates the principle of majority rule?

a. The First Amendment
b. The number of Senators
c. The Electoral College
d. Direct election of representatives

94. Which of the following BEST describes fiscal federalism?

a. The giving of federal funds to the states to help run programs
b. The giving of state funds to counties to help run programs
c. The concurrent power to raise funds through taxes
d. The concurrent power to establish fiscal policy

95. The Supreme Court case McCulloch v. Maryland helped establish

a. cooperative federalism.
b. dual federalism.
c. the authority of national law over state law.
d. the reserved powers of the states.

96. Which of the following is NOT a way Congress can check the power of the Supreme Court?

a. Rewriting laws ruled unconstitutional
b. Demoting the Chief Justice
c. Confirming new justices to the Court
d. Changing the number of justices

97. Which of the following is a main difference between a categorical grant and a block grant?

a. Categorical grants are more popular with states than the national government.
b. Block grants are awarded on a competitive basis, and categorical grants are not.
c. Categorical grants are issued with more spending restrictions than block grants.
d. Block grants are given only to state governments, and categorical grants are not.

98. According to the Tenth Amendment,

a. the people or states have powers that are not delegated to the national government.
b. the national government has powers not delegated to the states or people.
c. Congress has the power to regulate commerce between states.
d. states must give full faith and credit to the official acts of other states.

99. What is devolution?

a. The shifting of authority to state and local governments from the national government
b. The diffusion of power between many different state and local governments
c. The imposition of national laws on traditional state and local concerns
d. The inability to carry out national programs due to the decentralization of power

100. In Gibbons v. Ogden, the Supreme Court's ruling

a. broadly interpreted the commerce clause of the Constitution.
b. set a precedent for legal duties between states.
c. forbade the national government from outlawing slavery.
d. checked the power of the executive branch.

Answer Key and Explanations

1. B: Enumerated powers are powers specifically given to the government by the Constitution. Enumerated powers of Congress include the right to regulate commerce, establish posts offices, establish an army and a navy, collect taxes, and declare war, in addition to other powers. Congress also has implied powers, powers not expressly given to it by the Constitution. However, Congress does not have the power to appoint judges. The president has the authority to appoint federal judges, although the Senate has the power to confirm - or not to confirm - those appointments, itself a significant power.

2. C: Time allowed for debate is set by the Rules Committee in the House of Representatives. These time limits are then accepted by the majority of the entire House. The Senate allows more time to debate legislation; the House of Representatives is stricter in the sense that it typically has more rules than the Senate. Both the House and the Senate require bills to be reviewed by the relevant congressional committee first, before going (if at all) to the rest of Congress. This eliminates option D. The House is often more partisan than the Senate; this eliminates option A. The Senate does not have a Debate Committee; this eliminates option B.

3. A: Filibusters apply only in the Senate (this eliminates option B). Senators can extend debate indefinitely, until the bill's sponsors give up and withdraw the bill; this ensures that the legislation is never voted on and therefore does not become law. Filibusters are not used in committees. Instead, filibusters are used only after bills have left a relevant Senate committee and have come before the full Senate; this eliminates option C. Filibusters are not used to override vetoes; they are internal to the Senate rather than a check on the power of the president.

4. B: According to the trustee view of representation, representatives should look beyond the views of their constituents; they should also consider their own views and vote according to what they personally believe is right. In addition, according to this view, representatives should also consider what is best not only for their constituents, but what is best for the nation as a whole. This view is contrasted with a view of representation that regards representatives as instructed delegates, who are bound to vote as their constituents wish them to vote, regardless of the views representatives themselves hold. Only option B correctly describes the trustee view; the other options can be eliminated.

5. C: The majority party in Congress chooses the Speaker of the House and the Senate majority leader. Members of the majority party also serve as chairs of congressional committees, thereby leading and holding the majority of seats on those committees. Therefore, the majority party wields considerable power in Congress. However, the majority party cannot actually require party members to vote in certain ways (the majority power certainly wields influence on party members and exerts pressure, but it does not have the authority to actually require them to vote in certain ways).

6. D: Congress's oversight function is its function to monitor the executive branch in order to ensure that the executive branch is carrying out laws as Congress intends, as well as spending money in acceptable ways. The standing committees of Congress are important in carrying out the oversight function (for example, a standing committee on the judiciary, in both the Senate and the House, monitors the Department of Justice). Options A, B, and C each describe a way in which Congress carries out its oversight function. Congress does not fire officials in the executive branch, so option D is the correct answer.

7. A: A conference committee, composed of members of both the Senate and the House of Representatives, meets in order to agree on a compromise on new legislation, after the Senate and the House have passed different versions of the same legislation. Members of a conference committee are appointed by leaders of both political parties. Once the conference committee has agreed on a compromise, the new bill must be passed both by the full Senate and the full House of Representatives before it can become law. Only option A correctly describes the purpose of a conference committee.

8. B: Logrolling occurs when a legislator agrees to vote in a certain way in exchange for another legislator agreeing to vote in a certain way on a different matter. Logrolling is a way for two legislators both to get what they want. Legislators in the Senate do sometimes attach riders to bills, support bills that are favorable to wealthy interest groups, and (in the House especially) schedule voting on bills in a way that is most favorable to the majority party. However, none of these practices is the practice of logrolling.

9. B: In the House of Representatives, the Rules Committee can decide whether a bill – once it has gone to the full House for consideration – can be amended by the full House or not. If it can be amended, there is said to be an "open rule" regarding the bill; if it cannot be amended, there is said to be a "closed rule" regarding the debate. Imposing a closed rule is a way in which a majority party can limit the power of the minority party (because the minority party cannot change a bill it has doubts about; it can only debate and vote yea or nay). Option B is the only answer that correctly describes the purpose of introducing a bill under a closed rule.

10. D: Riders are amendments to a bill that are not related to the content of the bill. Such amendments can be added to a bill in the Senate, but not to bills in the House of Representatives. Regarding option A, the Speaker of the House has more formal power than the Senate majority leader (so option A is false). The House is also typically more partisan, not less partisan, than the Senate (so option B is false). Regarding option C, the Senate majority leader can add amendments to a bill (whether the Speaker of the House can depends on whether legislation was introduced under open or closed rules).

11. A: The House Rules Committee decides what bills to debate and when to debate them. This power is important because it gives the House Rules Committee the power to choose to schedule debate on a bill when the bill is likely to pass (or when the bill is likely not to pass, if the House Rules Committee chooses). Because the Speaker of the House appoints members to the House Rules Committee, the Committee is inclined to act in accordance with the Speaker's wishes. The House Rules Committee does not make appointments to standing committees. Nor does the House Rules Committee select the Speaker of the House (the Speaker is elected by the House of Representatives) or select who will speak during floor debate (a power that falls to the Speaker of the House).

12. C: The House of Representatives has the power to introduce bills that are about revenue (such as tax bills). This is the only option that correctly identifies a power the House of Representatives has that the Senate does not. The House of Representatives has the power to impeach, but it does not have the power to try officials who have been impeached (that power belongs to the Senate). So, option A can be eliminated. The Senate, not the House of Representatives, approves treaties and confirms (or chooses not to confirm) presidential appointments; so option D can be eliminated.

13. B: The Senate, not the House of Representatives, has the power to approve proposed treaties. The Senate tries government officials who have been impeached, but it does not itself impeach government officials (that is a power the House of Representatives has). This eliminates option A. Options C and D each describes a power the Senate has, but a power it shares with the House of

Representatives (as opposed to a power the Senate alone has). Congress as a whole provides oversight over the executive branch and has the power to declare war. Because these are shared responsibilities, options C and D can be eliminated.

14. C: In order for a bill to become law, the president must either sign the bill or fail to sign the bill while Congress is in session; if ten days pass without the president signing the bill and Congress remains in session during this time, the bill becomes law. However, if the president fails to sign the bill and Congress has finished its term, then the bill fails to become law. (If Congress wishes the bill to become law, it must start the legislative process again when Congress returns.) Option A is known as the line-item veto, not a pocket veto. A pocket veto does not concern signing statements or refusing to read the text of a proposed bill; therefore, options B and D can be rejected.

15. A: The president generally takes a leadership role over Congress in regard to national policy issues. In part this is because the powers and interests of Congress are somewhat decentralized: congresspersons serve constituents and might focus more on local interests rather than national interests. In addition, the committee system in Congress serves to help decentralize power (individual committees exercise considerable power over whether new bills even have the chance to become law). This places the president in a better position to focus on national policy. This does not mean that Congress always follows the wishes of the president on national policy; however, when the majority party is of the same party as the president, its agenda often broadly follows the policy of the president. All other options are false.

16. C: Executive privilege is the power of officials in the executive branch to keep information from Congress, even when appearing in official congressional hearings. It is also the power of such officials to refrain from appearing before congressional hearings in the first place. This power is not expressly given by the Constitution. Rather, it is thought to be an inherent power of the executive branch, and its limits and nature have been controversial. Options A, B, and C each describe powers of the executive branch (or of the president in particular), but do not describe executive privilege.

17. D: The president can issue executive orders about various matters. Often executive orders are regulations regarding carrying out law or abiding by the Constitution. Executive orders have the authority of law, although they are not passed by Congress, the legislative branch. For example, the Peace Corps was created through an executive order. The does serve as head of state, representing the nation as a whole; the president does not act as a legislator in this role. So option A can be eliminated. Similarly, the president also appoints diplomats and serves as commander-in-chief, but neither of these functions is specifically legislative (the former regards foreign relations, the latter military operations).

18. B: The president's ability to commit troops to action is limited by the War Powers Act, which requires Congress to approve the continued use of such troops after sixty days (that is, the president can keep troops in action for only 60 days before requiring the approval of Congress). Each other option enumerates a power the president possesses. Because the president has the power to recognize foreign governments as legitimate and negotiate treaties with other nations (though these treaties must be ratified by Congress), the president has authority over the nation's foreign policy.

19. C: The cabinet consists of government officials who are charged with leading the fifteen executive departments (such as the Department of Commerce, Department of Education, and Department of Defense). Sometimes a president will have an unofficial "kitchen cabinet" consisting of trusted advisers. The formal Cabinet no longer meets regularly with the president to provide advice on major policy issues facing the president, as its present size makes this impractical.

Cabinet members are appointed by the president and then confirmed (or not) by the Senate. Although option B correctly suggests that the Secretary of State and the Secretary of Defense are Cabinet members, the Senate majority leader is not officially a Cabinet member; so this option can be rejected.

20. A: Signing statements are statements presidents make when signing new legislation into law. Sometimes they are statements of how the president intends to carry out the law, directing executive agencies to specific ends. However, more recently, as with President George W. Bush, signing statements have more often been used to indicate that a president believes that the legislation (or aspects of the legislation) runs counter to national security or violates the Constitution. Because the Constitution directs the president to "faithfully execute" law, signing statements have been controversial. Only option A correctly describes signing statements.

21. D: The president cannot issue a pardon in the case of impeachment. However, the president has the authority to issue pardons in each of the other cases described by the other options. The president also has the authority to commute a sentence (lighten a convicted person's sentence). In addition, the president can offer reprieves, delaying the time when a convicted person's sentence is carried out. Sometimes presidential pardons have been controversial; for example, President Ford pardoned President Nixon for his involvement with the Watergate scandal, even before Nixon had been charged with any crime.

22. C: The Constitution gives the vice president little formal power (although the vice president becomes president if the president dies). However, the vice president formally presides over the Senate and can vote in the Senate if a vote is tied; so the vice president serves as a tiebreaker. This does not occur very often. Option C is the only option that correctly answers the question; the vice president cannot vote in the senate just because a senator is absent, for example, so option D can be rejected.

23. B: Capture refers to the tendency of regulatory agencies (for example, the Securities and Exchange Commission and the Environmental Protection Agency) to serve the interests of the industries they regulate, rather than providing objective oversight to serve public interests. One reason this might happen is because leaders in those industries provide information and advice to regulatory agencies, and sometimes that advice might be in the interests of the industry, not necessarily in the interests of the public; so, in following that advice, regulatory agencies serve the industries rather than the public. Regarding option C, the president does appoint individuals to lead and serve in regulatory agencies, but this is not what capture refers to.

24. C: Regulatory agencies have executive, legislative, and judicial powers. Regulatory agencies are given the power to regulate certain economic activities. Within an agency's field, an agency has the power to make rules (legislative power) and carry them out (executive powers). They also have the power to resolve disputes that arise concerning those rules (judicial powers). Regulatory agencies, then, are powerful agencies. Some are more independent of the president, and some are less so, depending in part on whether agency members can be dismissed at will by the president or serve a fixed term once appointed.

25. D: Government corporations share important similarities with private corporations. Government corporations (such as the United States Postal Service and Amtrak) can earn profits (nothing legally prevents them from doing so); this eliminates option A. Profits earned by government corporations are not taxed. They are overseen by a board of directors, like private corporations; this eliminates option B. In government corporations, the president appoints directors. They do receive federal funding; this eliminates option C. However, unlike private corporations, there are no stockholders in government corporations (one cannot buy shares in the United States Postal Service, for example).

26. A: According to the merit system in the civil service – service to the government –, individuals are hired, promoted, and fired at least in part on the basis of their performance on competitive examinations. This is meant to ensure that such individuals are competent and qualified, rather than acquiring government positions simply because they have personal connections or through political reasons. It is also meant to prevent corruption. It can be very difficult to fire a career civil servant. Because the merit system applies only to individuals – not entire departments – options C and D can be eliminated. Option B can be eliminated because according to the merit system, civil servants are not hired, promoted, or fired on the basis of work they did during political campaigns.

27. C: A sunset law is a law that will expire within a specified time period unless the law is re-authorized by Congress. This means that it is not up to the bureaucracy to decide whether a program under the law is worth carrying out; it is up to Congress. Congress does not often enact sunset laws. Congress does not have the power to dismiss civil servants; this eliminates option A. The Office of Management and Budget is under the president, not Congress; this eliminates option B. Similarly, the National Security Council is under the president, not Congress; this eliminates option D.

28. C: A whistleblower reports extreme mismanagement (or illegal behavior) by the government. Whistleblowers enjoy certain protections by law. For instance, the Office of Special Counsel (created by the Whistle-Blower Protection Act of 1989) investigates cases in which government employees complain that they have suffered retaliation at work in response to reporting mismanagement or legal wrongdoing. However, there are still relatively few whistleblowers. The other options are related in some way to whistle blowing (for instance, Congress might stop funding or conduct an investigation in response to what a whistleblower says), but they do not accurately describe whistle blowing itself.

29. D: The primary function of the bureaucracy is to put policy into place. It implements the policies of both the executive and legislative branches and sometimes rulings by the judicial branch as well. Sometimes there is tension between the policies of one branch and the policies of another branch (for instance, as when the political party of the president is the minority party in Congress rather than the majority power). Congress, the president, and the judiciary can each put a check on the power of the bureaucracies (in different ways), though the bureaucracy remains powerful. Option D is the only answer the correctly describes the relationship between the bureaucracy and the three branches of the federal government.

30. B: Independent executive agencies report directly to the president. However, they are not members of the president's cabinet; this eliminates option A. In addition, they are not run by a board of directors (as a government corporation is); this eliminates option C. Rather, they are run by an agency head that is appointed by the president. Independent executive agencies, like other agencies in the government, receive funding from the government, funding controlled by Congress (this is one way Congress exercises power over the bureaucracy). This eliminates option D.

31. A: An iron triangle consists of legislators, interest groups, and bureaucrats. The idea of an iron triangle is that policy within a given area (for example, agriculture) is formulated mainly by legislators working on that area, related interest groups, and bureaucrats in the federal government who help implement legislative policy. If applicable, the notion of an iron triangle illustrates the importance of interest groups in formulating policy. However, it has also been thought that the idea of an iron triangle presents a simplistic picture of policy-making today. Some thinkers believe that policy-making involves a more complicated network of individuals and interest groups.

32. A: Agenda setting is the power of the media to influence what issues the public believes are important by focusing news stories and commentary on those issues. In this way, the media can help shape public opinion, which then potentially influences government action and policy. The other options are also all related to the media: the media does "frame" stories by leaving out certain content related to a news story and including other content, for example (and it might do so to promote a certain political viewpoint); however, this is not agenda setting. Similarly, the media can serve as a watchdog over government practices and policies, but this is not agenda setting. Another important aspect of the media is that it allows government officials to communicate to the public; but this too is not agenda setting.

33. C: Interest groups use both the Internet as well as television, sometimes to promote particular candidates (among other things). Televised debates do help shape the perceptions of presidential candidates; a classic example of this was that Richard Nixon was widely perceived to have lost debates with John F. Kennedy, in part because Kennedy seemed confident and attractive, and Nixon did not (Nixon refused make-up prior to appearing on television, for instance). Contrary to option D, the government can prevent the publication of certain sensitive information (such as information related to troops in wartime). Studies have also shown that perception of media bias is often (not always) due to a person's own perspective rather than bias in the media itself.

34. D: Through enabling legislation, Congress creates an administrative agency to implement policy in a specific area. The legislation typically also spells out the name of the agency, how it is structured, and what the agency is authorized to do. Enabling legislation allows the national government to do more than it could otherwise; Congress itself cannot implement policy, and by creating an administrative agency to do so, it allows professionals in the relevant field to determine how best to implement the policies the national government has formulated in that field. All other options are incorrect.

35. C: By the original language of the Bill of Rights, the Bill of Rights applies only to the national government. That is, the Bill of Rights seems to forbid only the national government – not the state governments – from violating the rights specified in the Bill of Rights. Through incorporation, these rights are also understood to apply to state governments; that is, state governments are also forbidden to violate the rights specified in the Bill of Rights. Select incorporation is the application of specific rights specified in the Bill of Rights (not necessarily all of them) to state governments. The Fourteenth Amendment states that states cannot take away a person's life, liberty, or property without following the due process of the law. The Supreme Court interpreted the Fourteenth Amendment to justify applying certain rights in the Bill of Rights to state governments.

36. A: Through the power of judicial review, the Supreme Court rules on the constitutionality of the laws passed by Congress, as well as the constitutionality of actions taken by the President. This provides a check on the power of the legislative and executive branches of government by helping to ensure that they obey the Constitution. The power of judicial review was established by the court case Marbury v. Madison in 1803, when the Supreme Court was led by Chief Justice John Marshall. Prior to this case, it was not clear that the Supreme Court had this power, although the Constitution implied that it did. Since 1803, the Supreme Court has not often used this power in the sense that it has ruled relatively infrequently that the laws (or actions) taken by another government institution are unconstitutional.

37. D: The First Amendment guarantees freedom of speech, freedom of assembly, and freedom of religion. Freedom from unreasonable search and seizures is guaranteed by the Fourth Amendment. Due process – that one cannot be deprived of life, liberty, or property without the law being appropriately followed – is guaranteed in the Fifth Amendment. The freedom from having to incriminate oneself is also guaranteed by the Fifth Amendment. Although each possible answer to the question correctly identifies some rights guaranteed by the First Amendment, only answer D correctly identifies only rights that are guaranteed by the First Amendment.

38. B: The establishment clause in the First Amendment forbids the government from sponsoring any religion. A common interpretation of the clause is that it also forbids the government from favoring religion versus no religion. The government also cannot treat one religion better than another religion. The establishment clause provides the Constitutional basis for the separation between "church and state" – that is, between religion and the government. Thomas Jefferson described this division as a "wall of separation." Sometimes the establishment clause has been thought to conflict with the free exercise clause, which gives citizens the right to practice whatever religion they choose (or no religion, if they choose).

39. A: The 1962 case of Engel vs. Vitale (as well as in School District of Abington Township, Pennsylvania vs. Schempp) regarded the issue of students reciting prayers in school each morning in New York public schools. This practice, sanctioned by the State Board of Regents in New York, had been implemented in some such schools when it was challenged by parents. Although the parents initially lost their legal challenge to the practice, when the case reached the Supreme Court, the Supreme Court ruled in their favor, ruling that the school-sponsored prayer in a public school violated the First Amendment of the Constitution. In particular, the Court ruled that the practice violated the establishment clause, which forbids the government from establishing any religion as a state-sponsored religion. The case illustrates how the First Amendment is interpreted by the Supreme Court.

40. C: The case of Griswold v. Connecticut concerned a Connecticut law that made birth control devices illegal. The law was challenged and the Supreme Court ruled that the law was unconstitutional because it violated a right to privacy, the right of couples to make their own decisions about contraception. Although this right is not specified in the Bill of Rights, the Court reasoned that the Bill of Rights implied that there was such a right, that citizens have a "zone of privacy." The right to privacy was later invoked in the Court's ruling on abortion in the landmark case Roe v. Wade. At the time of Griswold v. Connecticut, it was controversial whether the Constitution guaranteed a right to privacy. That there is such a right in the Constitution is now established precedent.

41. D: Prior restraint refers to the fact that that the government cannot legally prohibit people or organizations from speaking or publishing prior to the fact – that is, before they have actually spoken or published. So, prior restraint prohibits censorship. (There are exceptions to this, as when censoring is overwhelmingly in the interests of national security; for example, the government can legally censor what the media says about the activities of the U.S. military when the nation is at war.) One case important to establishing prior restraint is the 1931 case of Near v. Minnesota. The state of Minnesota had shut down a newspaper after it was severely critical of government officials; the Supreme Court ruled that the newspaper must be allowed to open and operate.

42. B: According to the clear and present danger test, speech can be restricted if it presents a clear and present danger. This test was established in 1919 by the Supreme Court. Justice Oliver Wendell Holmes wrote that when words "are of such a nature as to create a clear and present danger that they will bring about the substantive evils that Congress has a right to prevent," they can be restricted. The case illustrates how the rights guaranteed by the First Amendment are shaped and interpreted by the Supreme Court. Since the establishing of the clear and present danger test, the test has since been modified in some rulings. In 1969, in Brandenburg v. Ohio, the Supreme Court broadened free speech, making it more difficult for the government to curtail speech legally.

43. A: The Fourteenth Amendment states that no state shall "deny any person within its jurisdiction the equal protection of the laws." So the Fourteenth Amendment specifically concerns state governments, not the federal government, nor private companies or organizations (therefore, options B, C, and D can be rejected). The Fourteenth Amendment has been used to end practices by state and local governments that discriminated on the basis of race, ethnicity, and gender. For example, in Brown v. Board of Education, the Supreme Court ruled that so-called "separate but equal" educational facilities are "inherently unequal" and therefore violated the equal protection clause of the Fourteenth Amendment.

44. D: The Supreme Court has original jurisdiction over cases that involve opposing state governments, as well as cases that involve foreign diplomats. (Original jurisdiction is the right to hear the cases for the first time, before other courts hear them.) This is the only option that correctly describes the extent of the Court's original jurisdiction. The Supreme Court hears many other sorts of cases (for instances, cases involving accusations of treason), but it hears them as an appellate court; that is, it hears them after other courts have already heard them. Most of the cases the Supreme Court hears are cases that have been heard by other courts already and that come to the Supreme Court when those courts' rulings are challenged.

45. A: The Supreme Court chooses among thousands of possible cases, selecting cases of especially substantive and significant legal issues, cases that are likely to have widespread or significant impact, depending on how the justices rule. The Court does not accept cases just on the basis that the justices believe that a lower court made a mistake; such a case might bear on a relatively insignificant issue, and then the Court is likely not to accept the case; the eliminates option D. Option B is too narrow; though the Court might well accept cases involving potentially unconstitutional uses of power, the Court decides to accept cases on broader grounds than these (grounds described by option A). When the Court chooses to review a case, it issues a writ of certiorari, which requires the relevant lower court to send information about the case to the Supreme Court. At least four justices must agree to review the case before the Supreme Court issues a write of certiorari.

46. C: According to the principle of stare decisis, judicial rulings should follow the precedents established by previous judicial rulings. That is, courts should rule in ways that are similar to how courts have ruled in the past when deciding similar kinds of cases. According to the principle of stare decisis, for example, lower courts should follow the precedents established by the Supreme Court. Option B can be eliminated because it is a narrower answer than option C. Although according to stare decisis, state courts should follow precedents established by the Supreme Court, stare decisis does not just involve state courts (it also involves lower federal courts). Because option C describes a fuller, and therefore more accurate description of stare decisis, option C is a better answer than option B.

47. B: U.S. District courts, federal courts below the Supreme Court, have a wide jurisdiction, meaning that they have the authority to hear a wide range of cases. Cases that involve charges of violations of both civil and criminal federal law are heard by U.S. District courts. Because district courts have this broad jurisdiction, this eliminates option A. Because U.S. District courts focus on federal law rather than state law, this eliminates option B. In addition to district courts, some federal courts focus on a particular area of law, such as bankruptcy.

48. C: A justice of the Supreme Court monitors each circuit of the federal appeals courts. Although justices of the Supreme Court often served as judges of appeals courts prior to serving as Supreme Court justices, there is no requirement for them to do so; this eliminates option D. The Supreme Court may well choose to review cases that have been heard by a federal appeals court; in fact, it might do so when different appeals courts rule differently in similar sorts of cases, in order to establish a more consistent legal interpretation. However, judges of the appeals courts do not compile a list of cases for potential review by the Supreme Court. Also, the Supreme Court, if it accepts cases heard by an appeals court, accepts such cases after, not before, they have been heard by an appeals court.

49. C: According to the view of judicial restraint, the judiciary should pay careful attention to the wording of the law, giving rulings according to a close reading of laws. In addition, the judiciary should show respect to other branches of government, according respect to legislatures and even the judgment of the executive branch over the judgment of officials in the judiciary branch. Judicial restraint is opposed to judicial activism, which can be understood as the view that the judiciary should exercise its power to ensure that other branches of government do not take unconstitutional or otherwise illegal action. Advocates of judicial restraint tend to place more emphasis on following legal precedents rather than interpreting law according to perceived current needs.

50. D: Appeals courts generally do not consider the facts of a case – that is, the particular circumstances involved in a particular case. It is often taken for granted that these are correct and that there is no need to review them further. Rather, appeals courts proceed by reviewing cases based on the records of the case of the lower court that heard the case. A panel of judges, usually numbering in three, reviews the records to look for legal errors. So, appeals courts do not involve juries at all in their decisions. This eliminates options A and B. The decisions of appeals courts are often final. If an appeals court ruling is challenged, the next step would be for the case to go the Supreme Court, and the Supreme Court agrees to hear few cases.

51. C: According to the Fourteenth Amendment, states cannot "deprive any person of life, liberty, or property without due process of law." Because the due process clause of the Fourteenth Amendment specifically concerns states, options A and B can be eliminated. Because the due process clause specifically concerns life, liberty, and property – not freedom of speech, religion, or assembly – option D can be eliminated. The due process clause is intended to protect individual rights by requiring state governments to follow appropriate legal procedures in the actions it takes.

52. D: Senatorial courtesy is the tradition that, when there is an opening for a judge in a federal district court, the president consults with the senator (or senators) of the state where the opening exists – provided that the senator or senators belong to the same party the president does. This has the effect of limiting the power of the president to make judicial appointments to federal district courts. If the president does not consult the senator (or senators), the senator (or senators) might oppose the president's nomination, with the rest of the senators following suit out of courtesy to the first senator; in that case, the president's appointee would not be confirmed. Option D is the only correct answer.

53. B: Both interest groups and political parties advance particular agendas (although interest groups' agendas are often narrower and their policy positions more specific than that of political parties). However, interest groups do not seek formal control of government operations; they do not themselves advance candidates for political office, whereas political parties do. Both interest groups and political parties have significant influence on legislation; this eliminates option A. Political parties often make heavy use of the media to promote candidates for political office; this eliminates option C.

54. D: The Democratic Party under General Andrew Jackson favored white Americans over African Americans (a trend that continued for some time). The Party was successful in part because it worked to get "common" people to vote and promoted the interests of the "common" man. This eliminates option A. The Democratic Party was also in favor of individual freedom and not expanded government or expanded federal spending (it was the Whig Party, opposed by the Democrats, which was more in favor of federal spending on infrastructure). This eliminates options B and C.

55. C: Republican President Hoover and his administration did not succeed in addressing the suffering caused by the Great Depression, at least not to the satisfaction of most citizens. Hoover believed that resolving the Great Depression was impossible through legislation, so his government played a limited role in addressing issues such as unemployment. Widespread dissatisfaction with his administration led to the election of Franklin Roosevelt and the rise of the Democratic Party for a time. The Democratic Party under Roosevelt did not take any significant steps regarding civil rights for minorities; many Southern Democrats would have opposed such steps. However, this was not the decisive factor in the political success of the Democratic Party (so option A can be eliminated).

56. A: A main purpose of political parties is to spell out policies on political issues. By doing so, they allow like-minded voters to mobilize to try to elect candidates who will work toward a given policy. A minority political party – the party that does not control the government – also spells out policies, and these serve as alternatives to the policies presented by the political party in power. Political parties do establish ties with interest groups, raise funds for political purposes, and try to attract widespread political support. However, these are not the main purposes of a political party; rather, they are actions a political party might take as it carries out its main purposes, such as spelling out policies and running political campaigns and elections.

57. B: At the national convention of a political party, the party formulates its platform and chooses it's presidential and vice presidential candidates. National parties do not select candidates for state office (they do not exercise that much power over state party organizations), so option A can be eliminated. Typically a national chairperson is not elected, but instead chosen by the party's presidential candidate (the party's national committee then ratifies the selection). This eliminates option C. National conventions do not explicitly select key candidates' positions, either through voting or anything else (rather, a candidate has usually already taken a stand on various policy matters well before the convention). A candidate for political office might take a position at odds with his or her party's official position, and the national committee has no authority to change the candidate's positions.

58. D: Economic groups have various advantages over citizens' groups. A main advantage is that economic groups have an easier time getting funding than citizens' groups. This is because they often, as businesses, make profits and are free to use those profits for lobbying purposes. In addition, they do not need to rely just on the goodwill of their members; a citizens' group often motivates members to contribute money by promoting a good the group believes is a good for all (such as a healthy environment); economic groups can often offer more tangible benefits (for instance, a union can offer a potential job with excellent benefits). All the other options are false; for instance, economic groups outnumber citizens' groups (so option B can be rejected).

59. A: A free rider is someone (or something) that enjoys a benefit without paying the cost of that benefit, or otherwise working for or contributing to that benefit. For example, everyone benefits from having cleaner air and water, and environmental interest groups might work to have them, relying on dues from their members to lobby the government. If they succeed in passing legislation that ensures cleaner air and water, everyone benefits from that legislation even though not everybody helped contribute to its passage. An individual might reason that such legislation will pass anyway, regardless of his or her support (because enough people will contribute funds). So, on one view, it is rational to keep one's own money (and not contribute) because one will get to enjoy cleaner air and water anyway. This kind of reasoning can make it difficult for citizens' groups to raise funds.

60. B: Each option describes a way in which interest groups lobby the government to promote regulations or legislation in their favor. However, only option B is an indirect way of lobbying. The other options are direct in the sense that they involve direct contact with government officials; for instance, a lobbyist for an interest group might provide both expertise in a given policy area, as well as information about how congressional representatives are likely to vote on a given bill. Holding mass demonstrations, however, is not an instance of directly interacting with the government, although it is an attempt to influence the government.

61. A: Inside lobbying involves techniques such as talking directly with government officials; lobbyists develop relationships with them and provide information and advice, and might even help draft legislation. Outside lobbying involves getting an organization's members to contact the government to express support for the interest group's favored position. So, outside lobbying is a way for an interest group to demonstrate that the interest group (or its position) has popular support and thus provide an incentive for the government to act in a way that the interest group favors. Outside lobbying can also involve seeking positive media attention; so, option B can be eliminated. Option D can be eliminated because inside lobbying, rather than outside lobbying, is used to establish closer relationships with legislators.

62. B: Interest groups donate political funds to individual candidates for political office through PACs. For candidates for political office at the federal level, a PAC can donate $5,000 during a primary election and another $5,000 during the general election, for a total of $10,000. These donation limits are set by federal law and do not necessarily reflect state laws. State laws regarding donations by PACs to candidates for political office vary; some set limits on the amount a PAC can donate to a single candidate, and some do not. Only option B correctly answers the question; all others can be eliminated.

63. D: Interest groups must typically have a lot of money to lobby the government successfully, and economic groups – which usually have more money than non-economic interest groups – significantly outnumber non-economic groups. As economic groups include groups such as corporation-based groups and groups based on industries and professions, this means that economic groups promoting the interests of (some of) the wealthy collectively have more influence than non-economic groups. Most members of Congress do receive PAC money from interest groups, and because campaigns are so expensive, those funds can play a significant role in a candidate's ability to run a successful campaign. These facts eliminate options A and C. There are not just a few interest groups with significant influence; especially influential groups include AIPAC, AARP, the NRA, and various labor and business groups.

64. A: PACs typically donate to incumbents, with whom interest group lobbyists have typically established a relationship and from whom the interest groups expect to benefit more. Incumbents do typically need PAC donations in order to run an effective, successful campaign for reelection; this eliminates option D. It is perfectly legal for PACs to donate to incumbents, so option C can be eliminated. PACs might even donate to incumbents whose views they are not entirely in favor of, out of a desire not to alienate incumbents if they win election (For a variety of reasons, incumbents are more likely to win than new candidates.).

65. A: In a pluralist theory in favor of interest groups participating in politics, interest groups serve an important purpose by representing diverse interests to the government; the people the government serves, after all – on this reasoning – is diverse as well, and different citizens desire different things. Interest groups help ensure that all interests are heard and, perhaps, acted on. The argument does not concern the power of interest groups relative to their number, nor the idea that interest groups somehow make government more cost-effective. This eliminates options B and D. Regarding option C, it seems to be true that interest groups have more influence on the government than ordinary citizens, but this is not the pluralist argument in favor of interest groups participating in politics.

66. A: In a blanket primary, voters can vote for either Republicans or Democrats (or, candidates of a minority party), even if the voters themselves are registered with one party or not registered at all. However, according to the Supreme Court, such primaries can be held only in elections that are not party-based in any way, on the grounds that otherwise selection of a party's candidate would depend partly on non-affiliated voters (robbing the party of the ability to choose its own candidate). Option B describes closed primaries. Options C and D do not describe blanket primaries.

67. D: State party organizations have central committees, the chairperson of which is responsible for the state party organization's daily operations. The chairperson is appointed by the central committee. Sometimes the governor or other elected official is the chairperson, but that need not necessarily be the case. Just as a party's national committee for the national organization accepts its presidential candidate's recommendation for chairperson, the central committee of a state party organization is likely to accept a governor's recommendation for chairperson (provided, of course, that the governor is of the same party), or the recommendation of some other high-level politician in the state.

68. C: Voters with lower incomes tend to vote more liberally on economic issues than voters with higher incomes, tending to favor government programs to help problems associated with lower incomes (such as government programs to boost employment). However, voters with lower incomes tend to vote more conservatively on social issues than voters with higher incomes; this eliminates option A. Because option C is true, option D must be false and can be rejected. Because voters with lower incomes tend to vote more conservatively than with the center on social issues, option B can rejected.

69. A: Voters who frequently attend church are more likely to vote Republican than voters who attend church less frequently. Of course, this does not mean that religious people never vote as Democrats, independents, or Libertarians. Some do. Other factors also affect voting behavior, such a person's family background, education, and peers. However, those who are more religious in the sense of frequently attending church are more likely to vote Republican than with any other political party in the United States, or as independents.

70. C: A sampling error is the difference between what the poll says public opinion is and what the poll would say if every single person who could have been polled actually was polled. So, a sampling error is an assessment of how accurate the poll is. The size of a poll affects its accuracy (a sample that is too small is unlikely to yield accurate results), and how people were selected to participate in the poll also affects its accuracy (if only drivers, for example, were polled, this would not represent the entire U.S. population, so a national poll that selected only drivers to participate might not yield accurate results). The wording of a poll also affects its accuracy – some wording might be biased or unclear and thus lead people to respond in a way that does not necessarily reflect their true views. However, only option C correctly defines sampling error.

71. B: A person's family upbringing is thought to be among the most important factors in what a person learns and comes to believe in politics. This need not mean that children never reject the political values and beliefs they learned from their parents. However, in many cases what people believe and value politically as adults was shaped by what they learned in their families, especially from parents. It makes sense that children would accept what their parents teach them, given the authoritative role that parents have and that most children desire parental approval. No other option correctly answers the question.

72. D: Civil disobedience is conscious disobedience of a law that the person breaking the law believes to be unjust. So it is not accidental disobedience to a law, but deliberate disobedience to make a political point, and is therefore one way individuals can participate politically. Answer C can be rejected because disobeying just any law in a nonviolent way need not count as civil disobedience (although civil disobedience is usually meant to be peaceful). For instance, peacefully refusing to pay a tax just because one would rather spend the money on something else (not because one believes the tax is unjust) does not count as civil disobedience. Answers A and B can be rejected because neither offers an accurate, general characterization of civil disobedience (for instance, civil disobedience does not necessarily involve demonstrating either for civil rights or civil liberties).

73. C: Although Republicans and Democrats can both be found in every region of the United States, the United States can also be understood as consisting of regions that are broadly Democratic and regions that are broadly Republican. Generally Democratic states are blue states and generally Republican states are red states. All of the options but C are regions where Blue states are concentrated; so, these options can be eliminated. The Rocky Mountains region is considered a region where red states are concentrated (although Colorado voted Democratic in the 2008 presidential election).

74. B: There tends to be a correlation between people's ages and their political views; this is known as the "lifestyle" effect. For example, younger people are often more liberal about social issues than older people, perhaps because older people hold on to values they had when they were younger (even if other segments of society begin to deviate from those values). For example, older people tend to be more concerned with issues such as the stability of Social Security than younger people. There are also correlations between political views and where one lives, one's education level, and one's economic status, but none of these correlations are the lifestyle effect.

75. D: Many people believe now that the media has become at least as important as the family in how people learn about politics. (The family itself is very important in how people learn about politics, including what people believe and value.) Some young people, for instance, cite the media more than they cite their families as sources of information about politics. The rise of the Internet and political comedy shows are also likely contributing factors to this trend. Option D is the only option that correctly answers the question.

76. C: It has been shown that sometimes people being questioned in a public opinion poll will make up an opinion rather than admit they don't have one about the issue at hand. This can skew the result of the poll, reflecting opinions people do not actually have. Polling, correctly done, is not inherently inaccurate, so option A can be rejected. If a sample does actually represent an entire population, that is likely to the make the poll more accurate, not less accurate, so option B can be rejected. Similarly, if the sample in a poll is random, that is also likely to make the poll more accurate, not less accurate, so option D can be rejected.

77. C: According to public opinion polls, sometimes the public has had a great deal of trust in the government, and other times not very much. Trust varies according to circumstances. In other ways as well, public attitudes about the government have varied; sometimes, for example, the notion that government was too small (and should not expand, or even be cut) was unpopular among the public, and other times (as when Ronald Reagan was president), popular among the public. People generally do, however, expect the government to address major problems in society, and people generally are strong supporters of the structure of the government (for example, its federalist and democratic features).

78. D: Exit polls are conducted by polling voters as they leave voting sites, asking how voters have voted. These are often done on election days. Exit polls have been controversial because sometime their accuracy has been questioned and because sometimes media will predict the winner of a race before all polling sites (where voters vote) in the country have closed; the concern is that this discourages voters in those areas from voting. Exit polls are not done by random telephone survey, or by asking about the effectiveness of specific officials, nor by asking people to evaluate an administration at the end of its term.

79. A: A president with strong support from the public is more powerful than a president with low support from the public. This is because Congress is more likely to try to work with a popular president to pass legislation (and grant funds) to do what the president wants; it is easier to say no to an unpopular president than a popular president. So public opinion can significantly affect the power of the president to get things done the president wants done. All other options are false. For example, studies show that public opinion does have an effect on the actions of the government (and not just during election years) and public opinion typically does not offer precise recommendations for government action; rather, it offers only general guidelines.

80. B: In some ways, women tend to vote in different ways than men and support different political positions. Women are more likely to vote for Democrats, for example, and they are more likely to support gay rights, affirmative action, and spending on social programs (such as welfare programs). They are more likely to oppose using military force and more likely to oppose capital punishment. These various differences are called the gender gap. It is not fixed; the pattern of voting and political preferences between men and women shows some variation.

81. D: Most Americans, even if they identify themselves as Democrats or Republicans (or as liberals or conservatives) are not consistently ideological. That is, their views do not consistently follow certain principles, such as the principle that government should stay small (or the principle that government should help people through social programs). More Americans identify themselves as conservatives than liberals, so option C can be rejected. Most Americans are not very informed about politics, so option A can be rejected. Most Americans do not often shift their allegiance from one political party to another (though party loyalty is not necessarily fixed, either), so option B can be rejected.

82. A: According to majoritarianism, government should do what the majority of people want it to do. Although this is a popular view of democracy, some people believe it does not necessarily describe how the United States government operates in practice. Some believe that, on the contrary, the government is actually run by an elite group of individuals who do not necessarily have the desires of the majority in mind. In addition, even if the government is not run by elites, it is not clear that the government can always do what the majority wants, simply because it is not always clear what the majority of people want. Answer A is the only answer that correctly describes the main idea of majoritarianism.

83. B: Shays' Rebellion consisted of armed farmers (led by Daniel Shay) revolting against the federal government. Under the Articles of Confederation, the government could not raise funds through the states, so it did not have the money to maintain an army. Accordingly, the rebellion illustrated that the central government was weak; it could not fight against armed revolt. Shays' Rebellion was related to the inability of the Congress to regulate commerce between states, but the Rebellion itself did not demonstrate that inability, so option D can be rejected.

84. D: The Great Compromise provided for a two-house system in Congress, consisting of a Senate and a House of Representatives. The number of representatives a state had in the House of Representatives would depend on how many people lived in that state; in the Senate, all states would have an equal number of representatives. Without this compromise, it is questionable whether smaller states would have agreed to the Constitution. In addition, by making the Senate in a way less representative than the House of Representatives, the Senate could check the power of the general public. This was a motivation as well. Although the delegates who formulated the Constitution did compromise regarding how slaves were to be counted for the purposes of determining a state's population, they did not compromise to protect the North's ability to limit slavery; nor was that a motivation in the Great Compromise.

85. B: The powers of the three branches of government (the executive, legislative, and judicial branches) are separate yet overlap. For instance, the president has the power to make certain judicial appointments, but Congress has the power to confirm – or choose not to confirm – those appointments. So the appointment of individuals to certain judicial positions is shared between the executive and legislative branches of the government. Regarding option C, it is true that the House and the Senate share legislative powers, but this is not the best description of the entire government's system of separation and powers, because it focuses only on the legislative branch and ignores the others (the executive branch shares legislative powers by its ability to veto legislation, for instance). Similarly, option D is too narrow, ignoring the judicial branch.

86. B: Madison argued that, unless a government operated under a system of checks and balances, there was a risk that a faction could dominate the government, counter to the public good. John Locke did not draft a theory of checks and balances; rather, one source for the idea is the French thinker Baron de Montesquieu. This eliminates option A. Madison was in favor of a strong national government, contrary to option C (though he also wanted to ensure that the government was not a tool for the "tyranny of the majority"). Finally, social contract theory played an important role in the history of the United States, but option D does not accurately describe why Madison advocated a system of checks and balances.

87. C: At the time American delegates drafted the Constitution, there was no nation with a federalist government. Some delegates were very concerned about the possibility of a strong national government becoming too strong and thereby threatening the power of the states and individual liberty. At the same time, many delegates recognized that the weak national government established by the Articles of Confederation was not sustainable. The decision to share power between a national government and state governments – a federalist structure – resulted as a compromise to resolve these concerns. The idea did not stem from the ideas of John Locke or Baron de Montesquieu.

88. A: A concurrent power is a power shared by the national government and the states. The states have police power, and the national government has police power as well (though it is somewhat limited). So police power is a concurrent power. The power to formulate foreign policy belongs only to the national government, so option B can be rejected. The power to regulate commerce between states also only belongs to the national government, so option C can be rejected. The power to regulate commerce strictly within a state is only a state power, so option D can be rejected.

89. D: Enumerated powers are powers specifically given to Congress by the Constitution. According to the elastic clause of the Constitution in Article I of the Constitution, Congress also has whatever powers are "necessary and proper" for carrying out those powers. The Constitution is the supreme law of the land, according to the Constitution, but that is not stated by the elastic clause, so option A can be rejected. The Tenth Amendment gives states "reserved powers," powers not given to the national government and that the Constitution does not forbid the states to have; therefore, option B can be rejected. The elastic clause does not state that the powers of Congress change according to circumstances, so option C can be rejected.

90. B: In cooperative federalism, the states and the national government jointly share funding, regulation, and implementation of a program or event. So a joint emergency response would be an instance of cooperative federalism. Option A does not address cooperative federalism, so it can be eliminated. States can form agreements between themselves, but this is not an instance of cooperative federalism, so option C can be rejected. States and national government do share tax powers, though they impose different kinds of taxes; in that sense, their powers are separate. However, this is not an instance of cooperative federalism (having different kinds of powers to tax does not itself illustrate joint funding, regulation, or implementation of any program).

91. C: In traditional democratic theory, a government should be arranged so that the rights of the minority cannot legally be infringed on by the majority. In the United States Constitution, the Bill of Rights helps ensure that this is the case (for instance, the minority has the right of free speech and the right to practice their own religion, even if what they have to say is not popular and even if very few people share their religion). All other options give an inaccurate description of the concept of minority rights in traditional democratic theory; the idea is not, for instance, that a one-person/one vote system typically protects the rights of the minority.

92. C: According to the pluralist theory of democracy, legislation is often passed through compromise. This is because, according to pluralism, the American democracy can be understood as a system in which different groups of people compete with each other for their own benefit. Because there are so many groups, they must work together to establish policy and create new laws (it is not possible for a single group to take control), and this often means compromising. Pluralists see this process as often benefiting the public good, not negatively affecting it, so option B can be rejected. Pluralism is based on the idea that a democratic society such as ours is very diverse, but it does not claim that democracy itself produces that diversity; this eliminates option A. Option D can be eliminated because pluralism denies that any one group or small groups dominates the government.

93. D: According to the principle of majority of rule, government should be run by the majority of people; it is the majority of the people who should choose government policy and decide who leads them, for example. The First Amendment does not address majority rule; rather, it provides limits on what the national government can do to its citizens, including citizens who belong to minority groups. The Electoral College is actually counter to the principle of majority rule, as it makes possible the election of presidents who did not receive the majority of votes. Similarly, the number of senators – 50 members, two for each state – is not the best illustration of the principle of majority rule, since it gives equal representation to all states, regardless of their population (so, the number of Senators tempers the power of the majority of people to choose national policy).

94. A: In fiscal federalism, the national government gives funds to the states so that states can carry out programs or projects; sometimes these programs are run jointly by states and the national government. National grants to states can come with strings attached; that is, the national government can put restrictions on how states spend the money. This is the only option that correctly describes fiscal federalism. The power to raise funds through taxes is a power shared by the states and the national government, but it does not describe fiscal federalism; so, option C can be rejected. The national government has the power to establish fiscal policy, but the power to establish fiscal policy is not a description of fiscal federalism; so, option D can be eliminated.

95. C: The case concerned whether the national government had the legal power to establish a national bank. The state of Maryland, in an effort to drive the national bank out of business, taxed the Maryland branch of the bank, which refused to pay. The Supreme Court, ruling that the national government did have the legal power to have such a bank, established that the national government, as long as it is abiding by the Constitution, is supreme over state law; in addition, it established that Congress has powers that are implied by the Constitution (such as the power to establish a national bank). The only correct answer to the question is C; the case did not establish reserved powers, or either cooperative or dual federalism.

96. B: Congress has the power to rewrite laws that the Supreme Court has ruled unconstitutional; so, the power of the Court is not absolute. Congress – in particular, the Senate – can also confirm, or choose not to confirm, appointments to the Supreme Court. In addition, it is not written in the Constitution that there must be nine justices on the Supreme Court, and Congress can increase or reduce that number (and sometimes it has). However, Congress cannot demote the Chief Justice of the Supreme Court, so option B is the correct answer.

97. C: The national government distributes block grants and categorical grants to both state and local governments, putting more restrictions on how the money can be spent in categorical grants than block grants. Giving funds in the form of categorical grants is one way the national government can influence states to behave in ways the national government wants. Because both sorts of grants are given to states and local governments, option D can be rejected. Block grants are not given on a competitive basis (though some categorical grants are), so option B can be rejected. Regarding option A, states tend to prefer block grants to categorical grants, because states have more discretion in spending the former; so option A can be rejected.

98. A: The Tenth Amendment reads in part, "The powers not dedicated to the United States by the Constitution, nor prohibited by it to the states, are reserved to the states respectively, or the people." So, according to the Tenth Amendment, the people or states have some powers that are not delegated to the national government (specifically, those that the Constitution also does not forbid the states from having). The Tenth Amendment has been interpreted as limiting the power of the national government, but it has also been interpreted as simply stating that states and the national government each have particular powers. How to interpret the Tenth Amendment matters because it concerns the issue of where states' rights end and the power of the national government begins – an issue that has historically been the focus of much debate (for example, the Civil War was at least partly a war about states' rights).

99. A: Devolution is the process of the shifting of authority to state and local governments from the national government. This process has occurred at various times in United States history – for example, under Reagan, who was a proponent of states' rights. The Supreme Court has also in recent years limited the national government's authority by more narrowly interpreting the commerce clause of the Constitution (the constitutional power of Congress to regulate commerce between states) than it had sometimes been interpreted before. However, the national government is certainly more powerful today than it was when it was first established, in part because what happens in one state often affects another (in other words, the dependency of states on each other helps make state issues national issues).

100. A: The case involved a dispute regarding whether a national government-issued license to operate steam-powered ferries in interstate waters permitted the license holder to do so in New York, or whether additional permission from New York was also required. Constitutionally, the case involved the interpretation of the commerce clause of the Constitution, a clause that gave Congress the power to regulate commerce between states, with Native American tribes, and with other nations. According to Chief Justice John Marshall's ruling, "commerce" meant all commercial activity (including navigation), thereby ruling that the national government had considerable regulatory authority over economic activity. (However, the ruling also held that the national government could not regulate commerce that occurred only within a single state.)

How to Overcome Test Anxiety

Just the thought of taking a test is enough to make most people a little nervous. A test is an important event that can have a long-term impact on your future, so it's important to take it seriously and it's natural to feel anxious about performing well. But just because anxiety is normal, that doesn't mean that it's helpful in test taking, or that you should simply accept it as part of your life. Anxiety can have a variety of effects. These effects can be mild, like making you feel slightly nervous, or severe, like blocking your ability to focus or remember even a simple detail.

If you experience test anxiety—whether severe or mild—it's important to know how to beat it. To discover this, first you need to understand what causes test anxiety.

Causes of Test Anxiety

While we often think of anxiety as an uncontrollable emotional state, it can actually be caused by simple, practical things. One of the most common causes of test anxiety is that a person does not feel adequately prepared for their test. This feeling can be the result of many different issues such as poor study habits or lack of organization, but the most common culprit is time management. Starting to study too late, failing to organize your study time to cover all of the material, or being distracted while you study will mean that you're not well prepared for the test. This may lead to cramming the night before, which will cause you to be physically and mentally exhausted for the test. Poor time management also contributes to feelings of stress, fear, and hopelessness as you realize you are not well prepared but don't know what to do about it.

Other times, test anxiety is not related to your preparation for the test but comes from unresolved fear. This may be a past failure on a test, or poor performance on tests in general. It may come from comparing yourself to others who seem to be performing better or from the stress of living up to expectations. Anxiety may be driven by fears of the future—how failure on this test would affect your educational and career goals. These fears are often completely irrational, but they can still negatively impact your test performance.

Elements of Test Anxiety

As mentioned earlier, test anxiety is considered to be an emotional state, but it has physical and mental components as well. Sometimes you may not even realize that you are suffering from test anxiety until you notice the physical symptoms. These can include trembling hands, rapid heartbeat, sweating, nausea, and tense muscles. Extreme anxiety may lead to fainting or vomiting. Obviously, any of these symptoms can have a negative impact on testing. It is important to recognize them as soon as they begin to occur so that you can address the problem before it damages your performance.

The mental components of test anxiety include trouble focusing and inability to remember learned information. During a test, your mind is on high alert, which can help you recall information and stay focused for an extended period of time. However, anxiety interferes with your mind's natural processes, causing you to blank out, even on the questions you know well. The strain of testing during anxiety makes it difficult to stay focused, especially on a test that may take several hours. Extreme anxiety can take a huge mental toll, making it difficult not only to recall test information but even to understand the test questions or pull your thoughts together.

Effects of Test Anxiety

Test anxiety is like a disease—if left untreated, it will get progressively worse. Anxiety leads to poor performance, and this reinforces the feelings of fear and failure, which in turn lead to poor performances on subsequent tests. It can grow from a mild nervousness to a crippling condition. If allowed to progress, test anxiety can have a big impact on your schooling, and consequently on your future.

Test anxiety can spread to other parts of your life. Anxiety on tests can become anxiety in any stressful situation, and blanking on a test can turn into panicking in a job situation. But fortunately, you don't have to let anxiety rule your testing and determine your grades. There are a number of relatively simple steps you can take to move past anxiety and function normally on a test and in the rest of life.

Physical Steps for Beating Test Anxiety

While test anxiety is a serious problem, the good news is that it can be overcome. It doesn't have to control your ability to think and remember information. While it may take time, you can begin taking steps today to beat anxiety.

Just as your first hint that you may be struggling with anxiety comes from the physical symptoms, the first step to treating it is also physical. Rest is crucial for having a clear, strong mind. If you are tired, it is much easier to give in to anxiety. But if you establish good sleep habits, your body and mind will be ready to perform optimally, without the strain of exhaustion. Additionally, sleeping well helps you to retain information better, so you're more likely to recall the answers when you see the test questions.

Getting good sleep means more than going to bed on time. It's important to allow your brain time to relax. Take study breaks from time to time so it doesn't get overworked, and don't study right before bed. Take time to rest your mind before trying to rest your body, or you may find it difficult to fall asleep.

Along with sleep, other aspects of physical health are important in preparing for a test. Good nutrition is vital for good brain function. Sugary foods and drinks may give a burst of energy but this burst is followed by a crash, both physically and emotionally. Instead, fuel your body with protein and vitamin-rich foods.

Also, drink plenty of water. Dehydration can lead to headaches and exhaustion, especially if your brain is already under stress from the rigors of the test. Particularly if your test is a long one, drink water during the breaks. And if possible, take an energy-boosting snack to eat between sections.

Along with sleep and diet, a third important part of physical health is exercise. Maintaining a steady workout schedule is helpful, but even taking 5-minute study breaks to walk can help get your blood pumping faster and clear your head. Exercise also releases endorphins, which contribute to a positive feeling and can help combat test anxiety.

When you nurture your physical health, you are also contributing to your mental health. If your body is healthy, your mind is much more likely to be healthy as well. So take time to rest, nourish your body with healthy food and water, and get moving as much as possible. Taking these physical steps will make you stronger and more able to take the mental steps necessary to overcome test anxiety.

Mental Steps for Beating Test Anxiety

Working on the mental side of test anxiety can be more challenging, but as with the physical side, there are clear steps you can take to overcome it. As mentioned earlier, test anxiety often stems from lack of preparation, so the obvious solution is to prepare for the test. Effective studying may be the most important weapon you have for beating test anxiety, but you can and should employ several other mental tools to combat fear.

First, boost your confidence by reminding yourself of past success—tests or projects that you aced. If you're putting as much effort into preparing for this test as you did for those, there's no reason you should expect to fail here. Work hard to prepare; then trust your preparation.

Second, surround yourself with encouraging people. It can be helpful to find a study group, but be sure that the people you're around will encourage a positive attitude. If you spend time with others who are anxious or cynical, this will only contribute to your own anxiety. Look for others who are motivated to study hard from a desire to succeed, not from a fear of failure.

Third, reward yourself. A test is physically and mentally tiring, even without anxiety, and it can be helpful to have something to look forward to. Plan an activity following the test, regardless of the outcome, such as going to a movie or getting ice cream.

When you are taking the test, if you find yourself beginning to feel anxious, remind yourself that you know the material. Visualize successfully completing the test. Then take a few deep, relaxing breaths and return to it. Work through the questions carefully but with confidence, knowing that you are capable of succeeding.

Developing a healthy mental approach to test taking will also aid in other areas of life. Test anxiety affects more than just the actual test—it can be damaging to your mental health and even contribute to depression. It's important to beat test anxiety before it becomes a problem for more than testing.

Study Strategy

Being prepared for the test is necessary to combat anxiety, but what does being prepared look like? You may study for hours on end and still not feel prepared. What you need is a strategy for test prep. The next few pages outline our recommended steps to help you plan out and conquer the challenge of preparation.

Step 1: Scope Out the Test

Learn everything you can about the format (multiple choice, essay, etc.) and what will be on the test. Gather any study materials, course outlines, or sample exams that may be available. Not only will this help you to prepare, but knowing what to expect can help to alleviate test anxiety.

Step 2: Map Out the Material

Look through the textbook or study guide and make note of how many chapters or sections it has. Then divide these over the time you have. For example, if a book has 15 chapters and you have five days to study, you need to cover three chapters each day. Even better, if you have the time, leave an extra day at the end for overall review after you have gone through the material in depth.

If time is limited, you may need to prioritize the material. Look through it and make note of which sections you think you already have a good grasp on, and which need review. While you are studying, skim quickly through the familiar sections and take more time on the challenging parts.

Write out your plan so you don't get lost as you go. Having a written plan also helps you feel more in control of the study, so anxiety is less likely to arise from feeling overwhelmed at the amount to cover.

Step 3: Gather Your Tools

Decide what study method works best for you. Do you prefer to highlight in the book as you study and then go back over the highlighted portions? Or do you type out notes of the important information? Or is it helpful to make flashcards that you can carry with you? Assemble the pens, index cards, highlighters, post-it notes, and any other materials you may need so you won't be distracted by getting up to find things while you study.

If you're having a hard time retaining the information or organizing your notes, experiment with different methods. For example, try color-coding by subject with colored pens, highlighters, or post-it notes. If you learn better by hearing, try recording yourself reading your notes so you can listen while in the car, working out, or simply sitting at your desk. Ask a friend to quiz you from your flashcards, or try teaching someone the material to solidify it in your mind.

Step 4: Create Your Environment

It's important to avoid distractions while you study. This includes both the obvious distractions like visitors and the subtle distractions like an uncomfortable chair (or a too-comfortable couch that makes you want to fall asleep). Set up the best study environment possible: good lighting and a comfortable work area. If background music helps you focus, you may want to turn it on, but otherwise keep the room quiet. If you are using a computer to take notes, be sure you don't have any other windows open, especially applications like social media, games, or anything else that could distract you. Silence your phone and turn off notifications. Be sure to keep water close by so you stay hydrated while you study (but avoid unhealthy drinks and snacks).

Also, take into account the best time of day to study. Are you freshest first thing in the morning? Try to set aside some time then to work through the material. Is your mind clearer in the afternoon or evening? Schedule your study session then. Another method is to study at the same time of day that you will take the test, so that your brain gets used to working on the material at that time and will be ready to focus at test time.

Step 5: Study!

Once you have done all the study preparation, it's time to settle into the actual studying. Sit down, take a few moments to settle your mind so you can focus, and begin to follow your study plan. Don't give in to distractions or let yourself procrastinate. This is your time to prepare so you'll be ready to fearlessly approach the test. Make the most of the time and stay focused.

Of course, you don't want to burn out. If you study too long you may find that you're not retaining the information very well. Take regular study breaks. For example, taking five minutes out of every hour to walk briskly, breathing deeply and swinging your arms, can help your mind stay fresh.

As you get to the end of each chapter or section, it's a good idea to do a quick review. Remind yourself of what you learned and work on any difficult parts. When you feel that you've mastered the material, move on to the next part. At the end of your study session, briefly skim through your notes again.

But while review is helpful, cramming last minute is NOT. If at all possible, work ahead so that you won't need to fit all your study into the last day. Cramming overloads your brain with more information than it can process and retain, and your tired mind may struggle to recall even previously learned information when it is overwhelmed with last-minute study. Also, the urgent nature of cramming and the stress placed on your brain contribute to anxiety. You'll be more likely to go to the test feeling unprepared and having trouble thinking clearly.

So don't cram, and don't stay up late before the test, even just to review your notes at a leisurely pace. Your brain needs rest more than it needs to go over the information again. In fact, plan to finish your studies by noon or early afternoon the day before the test. Give your brain the rest of the day to relax or focus on other things, and get a good night's sleep. Then you will be fresh for the test and better able to recall what you've studied.

Step 6: Take a Practice Test

Many courses offer sample tests, either online or in the study materials. This is an excellent resource to check whether you have mastered the material, as well as to prepare for the test format and environment.

Check the test format ahead of time: the number of questions, the type (multiple choice, free response, etc.), and the time limit. Then create a plan for working through them. For example, if you have 30 minutes to take a 60-question test, your limit is 30 seconds per question. Spend less time on the questions you know well so that you can take more time on the difficult ones.

If you have time to take several practice tests, take the first one open book, with no time limit. Work through the questions at your own pace and make sure you fully understand them. Gradually work up to taking a test under test conditions: sit at a desk with all study materials put away and set a timer. Pace yourself to make sure you finish the test with time to spare and go back to check your answers if you have time.

After each test, check your answers. On the questions you missed, be sure you understand why you missed them. Did you misread the question (tests can use tricky wording)? Did you forget the information? Or was it something you hadn't learned? Go back and study any shaky areas that the practice tests reveal.

Taking these tests not only helps with your grade, but also aids in combating test anxiety. If you're already used to the test conditions, you're less likely to worry about it, and working through tests until you're scoring well gives you a confidence boost. Go through the practice tests until you feel comfortable, and then you can go into the test knowing that you're ready for it.

Test Tips

On test day, you should be confident, knowing that you've prepared well and are ready to answer the questions. But aside from preparation, there are several test day strategies you can employ to maximize your performance.

First, as stated before, get a good night's sleep the night before the test (and for several nights before that, if possible). Go into the test with a fresh, alert mind rather than staying up late to study.

Try not to change too much about your normal routine on the day of the test. It's important to eat a nutritious breakfast, but if you normally don't eat breakfast at all, consider eating just a protein bar. If you're a coffee drinker, go ahead and have your normal coffee. Just make sure you time it so that the caffeine doesn't wear off right in the middle of your test. Avoid sugary beverages, and drink enough water to stay hydrated but not so much that you need a restroom break 10 minutes into the test. If your test isn't first thing in the morning, consider going for a walk or doing a light workout before the test to get your blood flowing.

Allow yourself enough time to get ready, and leave for the test with plenty of time to spare so you won't have the anxiety of scrambling to arrive in time. Another reason to be early is to select a good seat. It's helpful to sit away from doors and windows, which can be distracting. Find a good seat, get out your supplies, and settle your mind before the test begins.

When the test begins, start by going over the instructions carefully, even if you already know what to expect. Make sure you avoid any careless mistakes by following the directions.

Then begin working through the questions, pacing yourself as you've practiced. If you're not sure on an answer, don't spend too much time on it, and don't let it shake your confidence. Either skip it and come back later, or eliminate as many wrong answers as possible and guess among the remaining ones. Don't dwell on these questions as you continue—put them out of your mind and focus on what lies ahead.

Be sure to read all of the answer choices, even if you're sure the first one is the right answer. Sometimes you'll find a better one if you keep reading. But don't second-guess yourself if you do immediately know the answer. Your gut instinct is usually right. Don't let test anxiety rob you of the information you know.

If you have time at the end of the test (and if the test format allows), go back and review your answers. Be cautious about changing any, since your first instinct tends to be correct, but make sure you didn't misread any of the questions or accidentally mark the wrong answer choice. Look over any you skipped and make an educated guess.

At the end, leave the test feeling confident. You've done your best, so don't waste time worrying about your performance or wishing you could change anything. Instead, celebrate the successful completion of this test. And finally, use this test to learn how to deal with anxiety even better next time.

Review Video: Test Anxiety
Visit mometrix.com/academy and enter code: 100340

Important Qualification

Not all anxiety is created equal. If your test anxiety is causing major issues in your life beyond the classroom or testing center, or if you are experiencing troubling physical symptoms related to your anxiety, it may be a sign of a serious physiological or psychological condition. If this sounds like your situation, we strongly encourage you to seek professional help.

Online Resources

Due to our efforts to try to keep this book to a manageable length, we've created a link that will give you access to all of your online resources:

mometrix.com/resources719/clepamergov

It's Your Moment, Let's Celebrate It!

Share your story @mometrixtestpreparation